# TEACHER'S PET PUBLICATIONS

PUZZLE PACK
for
Of Mice and Men
based on the book by
John Steinbeck

Written by
William T. Collins

© 2005 Teacher's Pet Publications
All Rights Reserved

The materials in this packet are copyrighted
by Teacher's Pet Publications, Inc.

These pages may be duplicated by the purchaser
for use in the purchaser's own classroom.

Copying any of these materials and distributing them
for any other purpose is a violation of the copyright laws.

© 2005 Teacher's Pet Publications, Inc.
www.tpet.com

INTRODUCTION
If you already own the LitPlan for this title, this Puzzle Pack will refresh your Unit Resource Materials and Vocabulary Resource Materials sections plus give you additional materials you can substitute into the tests. If you do not already have a complete LitPlan, these pages will give you some supplemental materials to use with your own plan. There are two main groups of materials: one set for unit words (such as characters' names, symbols, places, etc.) and one set for vocabulary words associated with the book.

WORD LIST
There is a word list for both the unit words and the vocabulary words. These lists show you which words are being used in the materials and the clues or definitions being used for those words. You may want to give students a word list with clues/definitions to help them, or you may want students to only have a word list (without clues/definitions) if you want them to work a little harder. Both are available for duplication. The word lists can also be your "calling key" for the bingo games.

FILL IN THE BLANK AND MATCHING
There are 4 each of the fill in the blank and matching worksheets for both the unit and vocabulary words. These pages can be used either as extra worksheets for students or as objective parts of a unit test. They can be done individually if students need extra help or as a whole class activity to review the material covered.

MAGIC SQUARES
The magic squares not only reinforce the material covered but also work on reasoning and math skills. Many teachers have told us that their students really enjoy doing these!

WORD SEARCH PUZZLES
The word search words go in all directions, as indicated on your answer keys. Two of the word search puzzles have the clues listed rather than the words. This makes the puzzle a little more difficult, but it reinforces the material better. Two word search puzzles have words only for students who find the clue puzzles too difficult.

CROSSWORD PUZZLES
Both unit and vocabulary word sections have 4 crossword puzzles.

BINGO CARDS
There are 32 individual bingo cards for the unit words and 32 individual bingo cards for the vocabulary words. You can use your word list as a "call list," calling the words at random and marking them off of your list as you go, or you could use the flash cards by cutting them apart and drawing the words at random from a hat (or box or whatever). To make a better review, you might ask for the definition and spelling of each word as you call it out–or you could call out the definitions and have students tell you the words they need to look for on the puzzle.

JUGGLE LETTERS
The vocabulary juggle letter game is intended to help students learn the spellings of the words. One sheet has the definitions listed on it as an extra help for students who need it or to reinforce the definitions if you choose to do so.

FLASH CARDS
We've included a set of vocabulary flash cards you can duplicate, cut, and fold for your students. Some teachers make a few sets for general use by the class; others make a set for each student. Some teachers duplicate them for each student and have the students cut & fold their own. You can cut out just the words and put them in a hat, have each student pick out one word and write the definition and a sentence for that word. Students then swap words and papers, with the next student adding a sentence of his own under the last one. You can have students swap as many times as you like. Each time the student will read the sentences written prior to his own and then add a sentence. You can cut out the words and definitions separately and play "I Have; Who Has?" Each student in the room draws a word and definition. The first student says, "I have (the name of the word). Who has the definition?" The student with the definition reads it then says, "I have (the name of the vocabulary word she has). Who has the definition?" The round continues until all words and definitions have been given.

Of Mice and Men Word List

No.	Word	Clue/Definition
1.	BAD	I done a ___ thing. I done another ___ thing.
2.	BARN	Place to keep animals and store hay
3.	BEANS	George had 4 cans of these to eat; Lennie liked ketchup on his
4.	BINDLE	Slang for a ranch hand's bedroll
5.	BOSS	One in charge
6.	BUNK	Ranch hand's bed
7.	CAMPSITE	Outdoor place ranchers stay overnight
8.	CANDY	Old swamper whose dog was killed
9.	CARLSON	Killed Candy's dog
10.	CAVE	Lennie offers to go away and live in one.
11.	CLARA	Lennie's aunt who gave him mice
12.	COMPLAIN	George always ___s about Lennie.
13.	CROOKS	Stable man
14.	CURLEY	Ill-tempered son of the ranch owner
15.	FIGHT	What Curley likes to do
16.	FORGOT	Lennie often did this; didn't remember.
17.	FRIENDS	George and Lennie, for example
18.	FUTURE	With us it ain't like that. We got a ___.
19.	GEORGE	He killed Lennie.
20.	GLOVE	Curley wore one on his left hand.
21.	HAND	Lennie crushed Curley's
22.	HEAVEN	Nobody gets to ___ and nobody gets no land.
23.	JAIL	She's ___ bait all set on the trigger.
24.	LAND	What George and Lennie hope to own someday
25.	LENNIE	He is mentally slow but physically strong.
26.	LUGER	George shot Lennie with it.
27.	MILTON	George's last name
28.	MOUSE	Lennie carried a dead one in his pocket.
29.	NECK	Lennie breaks Curley's wife's
30.	PET	What Lennie liked to do to the dead mouse
31.	PUPPIES	What Slim has that Lennie wants
32.	RABBITS	What Lennie wants to tend someday
33.	RAPE	Lennie was accused of this in Weed.
34.	SALINAS	A few miles south of Soledad, this river runs deep and green.
35.	SENSE	Guy don't need no ___ to be a nice fella
36.	SICK	I tell ya a guy gets too lonely an' he gets ___.
37.	SLIM	Ranch foreman
38.	SMALL	Lennie's last name
39.	SOLITAIRE	Card game George plays
40.	STEINBECK	Author
41.	TRAMP	Curley's wife acts like one.
42.	WEED	Town George and Lennie had to leave.

Of Mice and Men Fill In The Blanks 1

_____   1. Town George and Lennie had to leave.
_____   2. Stable man
_____   3. He is mentally slow but physically strong.
_____   4. Lennie was accused of this in Weed.
_____   5. Lennie carried a dead one in his pocket.
_____   6. She's ___ bait all set on the trigger.
_____   7. Card game George plays
_____   8. With us it ain't like that. We got a ___.
_____   9. Killed Candy's dog
_____   10. George and Lennie, for example
_____   11. Lennie often did this; didn't remember.
_____   12. Lennie's aunt who gave him mice
_____   13. Lennie offers to go away and live in one.
_____   14. Guy don't need no ___ to be a nice fella
_____   15. One in charge
_____   16. Ill-tempered son of the ranch owner
_____   17. George shot Lennie with it.
_____   18. He killed Lennie.
_____   19. George always ____s about Lennie.
_____   20. Curley wore one on his left hand.

Of Mice and Men Fill In The Blanks 1 Answer Key

WEED	1. Town George and Lennie had to leave.
CROOKS	2. Stable man
LENNIE	3. He is mentally slow but physically strong.
RAPE	4. Lennie was accused of this in Weed.
MOUSE	5. Lennie carried a dead one in his pocket.
JAIL	6. She's ___ bait all set on the trigger.
SOLITAIRE	7. Card game George plays
FUTURE	8. With us it ain't like that. We got a ___.
CARLSON	9. Killed Candy's dog
FRIENDS	10. George and Lennie, for example
FORGOT	11. Lennie often did this; didn't remember.
CLARA	12. Lennie's aunt who gave him mice
CAVE	13. Lennie offers to go away and live in one.
SENSE	14. Guy don't need no ___ to be a nice fella
BOSS	15. One in charge
CURLEY	16. Ill-tempered son of the ranch owner
LUGER	17. George shot Lennie with it.
GEORGE	18. He killed Lennie.
COMPLAIN	19. George always ____s about Lennie.
GLOVE	20. Curley wore one on his left hand.

Of Mice and Men Fill In The Blanks 2

_____
_____
_____
_____
_____
_____
_____
_____
_____
_____
_____
_____
_____
_____
_____
_____
_____
_____
_____
_____

1. Lennie was accused of this in Weed.
2. What Curley likes to do
3. George shot Lennie with it.
4. He killed Lennie.
5. Author
6. A few miles south of Soledad, this river runs deep and green.
7. What Slim has that Lennie wants
8. Stable man
9. Lennie offers to go away and live in one.
10. Slang for a ranch hand's bedroll
11. I tell ya a guy gets too lonely an' he gets ___.
12. What George and Lennie hope to own someday
13. Nobody gets to ___ and nobody gets no land.
14. Lennie carried a dead one in his pocket.
15. Old swamper whose dog was killed
16. Lennie often did this; didn't remember.
17. Curley's wife acts like one.
18. I done a ___ thing. I done another ___ thing.
19. George always ____s about Lennie.
20. Card game George plays

Of Mice and Men Fill In The Blanks 2 Answer Key

Answer	#	Clue
RAPE	1.	Lennie was accused of this in Weed.
FIGHT	2.	What Curley likes to do
LUGER	3.	George shot Lennie with it.
GEORGE	4.	He killed Lennie.
STEINBECK	5.	Author
SALINAS	6.	A few miles south of Soledad, this river runs deep and green.
PUPPIES	7.	What Slim has that Lennie wants
CROOKS	8.	Stable man
CAVE	9.	Lennie offers to go away and live in one.
BINDLE	10.	Slang for a ranch hand's bedroll
SICK	11.	I tell ya a guy gets too lonely an' he gets ___.
LAND	12.	What George and Lennie hope to own someday
HEAVEN	13.	Nobody gets to ___ and nobody gets no land.
MOUSE	14.	Lennie carried a dead one in his pocket.
CANDY	15.	Old swamper whose dog was killed
FORGOT	16.	Lennie often did this; didn't remember.
TRAMP	17.	Curley's wife acts like one.
BAD	18.	I done a ___ thing. I done another ___ thing.
COMPLAIN	19.	George always ___s about Lennie.
SOLITAIRE	20.	Card game George plays

Of Mice and Men Fill In The Blanks 3

_____ 1. Outdoor place ranchers stay overnight

_____ 2. Card game George plays

_____ 3. Ill-tempered son of the ranch owner

_____ 4. She's ___ bait all set on the trigger.

_____ 5. Lennie carried a dead one in his pocket.

_____ 6. Lennie breaks Curley's wife's

_____ 7. He is mentally slow but physically strong.

_____ 8. I done a ___ thing. I done another ___ thing.

_____ 9. Stable man

_____ 10. Ranch hand's bed

_____ 11. Killed Candy's dog

_____ 12. A few miles south of Soledad, this river runs deep and green.

_____ 13. He killed Lennie.

_____ 14. Ranch foreman

_____ 15. Curley's wife acts like one.

_____ 16. Lennie's aunt who gave him mice

_____ 17. What George and Lennie hope to own someday

_____ 18. Town George and Lennie had to leave.

_____ 19. Nobody gets to ___ and nobody gets no land.

_____ 20. Guy don't need no ___ to be a nice fella

Of Mice and Men Fill In The Blanks 3 Answer Key

CAMPSITE	1. Outdoor place ranchers stay overnight
SOLITAIRE	2. Card game George plays
CURLEY	3. Ill-tempered son of the ranch owner
JAIL	4. She's ___ bait all set on the trigger.
MOUSE	5. Lennie carried a dead one in his pocket.
NECK	6. Lennie breaks Curley's wife's
LENNIE	7. He is mentally slow but physically strong.
BAD	8. I done a ___ thing. I done another ___ thing.
CROOKS	9. Stable man
BUNK	10. Ranch hand's bed
CARLSON	11. Killed Candy's dog
SALINAS	12. A few miles south of Soledad, this river runs deep and green.
GEORGE	13. He killed Lennie.
SLIM	14. Ranch foreman
TRAMP	15. Curley's wife acts like one.
CLARA	16. Lennie's aunt who gave him mice
LAND	17. What George and Lennie hope to own someday
WEED	18. Town George and Lennie had to leave.
HEAVEN	19. Nobody gets to ___ and nobody gets no land.
SENSE	20. Guy don't need no ___ to be a nice fella

Of Mice and Men Fill In The Blanks 4

_____

1. He killed Lennie.
2. Stable man
3. What Lennie liked to do to the dead mouse
4. With us it ain't like that. We got a ___.
5. What Curley likes to do
6. Lennie offers to go away and live in one.
7. Lennie breaks Curley's wife's
8. Lennie's last name
9. Lennie was accused of this in Weed.
10. George always ____s about Lennie.
11. Guy don't need no ___ to be a nice fella
12. She's ___ bait all set on the trigger.
13. George's last name
14. Town George and Lennie had to leave.
15. I done a ___ thing. I done another ___ thing.
16. One in charge
17. Nobody gets to ___ and nobody gets no land.
18. Ranch hand's bed
19. Lennie's aunt who gave him mice
20. Card game George plays

Of Mice and Men Fill In The Blanks 4 Answer Key

GEORGE	1. He killed Lennie.
CROOKS	2. Stable man
PET	3. What Lennie liked to do to the dead mouse
FUTURE	4. With us it ain't like that. We got a ___.
FIGHT	5. What Curley likes to do
CAVE	6. Lennie offers to go away and live in one.
NECK	7. Lennie breaks Curley's wife's
SMALL	8. Lennie's last name
RAPE	9. Lennie was accused of this in Weed.
COMPLAIN	10. George always ____s about Lennie.
SENSE	11. Guy don't need no ___ to be a nice fella
JAIL	12. She's ___ bait all set on the trigger.
MILTON	13. George's last name
WEED	14. Town George and Lennie had to leave.
BAD	15. I done a ___ thing. I done another ___ thing.
BOSS	16. One in charge
HEAVEN	17. Nobody gets to ___ and nobody gets no land.
BUNK	18. Ranch hand's bed
CLARA	19. Lennie's aunt who gave him mice
SOLITAIRE	20. Card game George plays

Of Mice and Men Matching 1

___ 1. BARN   A. Lennie's aunt who gave him mice
___ 2. TRAMP   B. Author
___ 3. STEINBECK   C. What Slim has that Lennie wants
___ 4. SMALL   D. George and Lennie, for example
___ 5. RAPE   E. What George and Lennie hope to own someday
___ 6. GLOVE   F. Lennie often did this; didn't remember.
___ 7. CROOKS   G. Curley's wife acts like one.
___ 8. FRIENDS   H. Ranch foreman
___ 9. PUPPIES   I. I done a ___ thing. I done another ___ thing.
___10. FORGOT   J. Ranch hand's bed
___11. SALINAS   K. Slang for a ranch hand's bedroll
___12. CURLEY   L. Curley wore one on his left hand.
___13. BINDLE   M. Town George and Lennie had to leave.
___14. LAND   N. George always ____s about Lennie.
___15. BAD   O. He killed Lennie.
___16. CAMPSITE   P. What Curley likes to do
___17. CLARA   Q. One in charge
___18. SENSE   R. Outdoor place ranchers stay overnight
___19. BUNK   S. Guy don't need no ___ to be a nice fella
___20. SLIM   T. Stable man
___21. GEORGE   U. Place to keep animals and store hay
___22. BOSS   V. Ill-tempered son of the ranch owner
___23. COMPLAIN   W. Lennie's last name
___24. WEED   X. Lennie was accused of this in Weed.
___25. FIGHT   Y. A few miles south of Soledad, this river runs deep and green.

Of Mice and Men Matching 1 Answer Key

- U - 1. BARN
- G - 2. TRAMP
- B - 3. STEINBECK
- W - 4. SMALL
- X - 5. RAPE
- L - 6. GLOVE
- T - 7. CROOKS
- D - 8. FRIENDS
- C - 9. PUPPIES
- F - 10. FORGOT
- Y - 11. SALINAS
- V - 12. CURLEY
- K - 13. BINDLE
- E - 14. LAND
- I - 15. BAD
- R - 16. CAMPSITE
- A - 17. CLARA
- S - 18. SENSE
- J - 19. BUNK
- H - 20. SLIM
- O - 21. GEORGE
- Q - 22. BOSS
- N - 23. COMPLAIN
- M - 24. WEED
- P - 25. FIGHT

A. Lennie's aunt who gave him mice
B. Author
C. What Slim has that Lennie wants
D. George and Lennie, for example
E. What George and Lennie hope to own someday
F. Lennie often did this; didn't remember.
G. Curley's wife acts like one.
H. Ranch foreman
I. I done a ___ thing. I done another ___ thing.
J. Ranch hand's bed
K. Slang for a ranch hand's bedroll
L. Curley wore one on his left hand.
M. Town George and Lennie had to leave.
N. George always ___s about Lennie.
O. He killed Lennie.
P. What Curley likes to do
Q. One in charge
R. Outdoor place ranchers stay overnight
S. Guy don't need no ___ to be a nice fella
T. Stable man
U. Place to keep animals and store hay
V. Ill-tempered son of the ranch owner
W. Lennie's last name
X. Lennie was accused of this in Weed.
Y. A few miles south of Soledad, this river runs deep and green.

Of Mice and Men Matching 2

___ 1. SENSE   A. Curley's wife acts like one.
___ 2. LENNIE   B. Lennie offers to go away and live in one.
___ 3. MOUSE   C. Town George and Lennie had to leave.
___ 4. SOLITAIRE   D. Ranch hand's bed
___ 5. PET   E. Lennie was accused of this in Weed.
___ 6. MILTON   F. Lennie's aunt who gave him mice
___ 7. TRAMP   G. George and Lennie, for example
___ 8. CARLSON   H. What Lennie liked to do to the dead mouse
___ 9. SLIM   I. He killed Lennie.
___10. BINDLE   J. George always ____s about Lennie.
___11. RAPE   K. George's last name
___12. SICK   L. Slang for a ranch hand's bedroll
___13. CROOKS   M. What Slim has that Lennie wants
___14. COMPLAIN   N. Killed Candy's dog
___15. PUPPIES   O. Place to keep animals and store hay
___16. CAVE   P. He is mentally slow but physically strong.
___17. GEORGE   Q. Lennie carried a dead one in his pocket.
___18. LAND   R. Ranch foreman
___19. WEED   S. Lennie breaks Curley's wife's
___20. CLARA   T. She's ___ bait all set on the trigger.
___21. FRIENDS   U. What George and Lennie hope to own someday
___22. JAIL   V. Stable man
___23. BARN   W. Card game George plays
___24. NECK   X. Guy don't need no ___ to be a nice fella
___25. BUNK   Y. I tell ya a guy gets too lonely an' he gets ___.

15
Copyrighted

Of Mice and Men Matching 2 Answer Key

X - 1. SENSE	A. Curley's wife acts like one.
P - 2. LENNIE	B. Lennie offers to go away and live in one.
Q - 3. MOUSE	C. Town George and Lennie had to leave.
W - 4. SOLITAIRE	D. Ranch hand's bed
H - 5. PET	E. Lennie was accused of this in Weed.
K - 6. MILTON	F. Lennie's aunt who gave him mice
A - 7. TRAMP	G. George and Lennie, for example
N - 8. CARLSON	H. What Lennie liked to do to the dead mouse
R - 9. SLIM	I. He killed Lennie.
L - 10. BINDLE	J. George always ____s about Lennie.
E - 11. RAPE	K. George's last name
Y - 12. SICK	L. Slang for a ranch hand's bedroll
V - 13. CROOKS	M. What Slim has that Lennie wants
J - 14. COMPLAIN	N. Killed Candy's dog
M - 15. PUPPIES	O. Place to keep animals and store hay
B - 16. CAVE	P. He is mentally slow but physically strong.
I - 17. GEORGE	Q. Lennie carried a dead one in his pocket.
U - 18. LAND	R. Ranch foreman
C - 19. WEED	S. Lennie breaks Curley's wife's
F - 20. CLARA	T. She's ___ bait all set on the trigger.
G - 21. FRIENDS	U. What George and Lennie hope to own someday
T - 22. JAIL	V. Stable man
O - 23. BARN	W. Card game George plays
S - 24. NECK	X. Guy don't need no ___ to be a nice fella
D - 25. BUNK	Y. I tell ya a guy gets too lonely an' he gets ___.

Of Mice and Men Matching 3

___ 1. RABBITS   A. George always ____s about Lennie.
___ 2. COMPLAIN   B. Town George and Lennie had to leave.
___ 3. MILTON   C. Lennie often did this; didn't remember.
___ 4. CAVE   D. Lennie breaks Curley's wife's
___ 5. CURLEY   E. What Lennie liked to do to the dead mouse
___ 6. CROOKS   F. What Lennie wants to tend someday
___ 7. BINDLE   G. Lennie was accused of this in Weed.
___ 8. NECK   H. Ranch foreman
___ 9. TRAMP   I. Slang for a ranch hand's bedroll
___10. SLIM   J. Stable man
___11. FORGOT   K. Curley's wife acts like one.
___12. LENNIE   L. Guy don't need no ___ to be a nice fella
___13. CARLSON   M. Lennie carried a dead one in his pocket.
___14. HEAVEN   N. Old swamper whose dog was killed
___15. FIGHT   O. He is mentally slow but physically strong.
___16. RAPE   P. George's last name
___17. STEINBECK   Q. What Slim has that Lennie wants
___18. MOUSE   R. Killed Candy's dog
___19. WEED   S. Lennie offers to go away and live in one.
___20. FRIENDS   T. Ill-tempered son of the ranch owner
___21. PET   U. George and Lennie, for example
___22. CANDY   V. Author
___23. PUPPIES   W. Place to keep animals and store hay
___24. SENSE   X. What Curley likes to do
___25. BARN   Y. Nobody gets to ___ and nobody gets no land.

Of Mice and Men Matching 3 Answer Key

F - 1. RABBITS	A.	George always ____s about Lennie.
A - 2. COMPLAIN	B.	Town George and Lennie had to leave.
P - 3. MILTON	C.	Lennie often did this; didn't remember.
S - 4. CAVE	D.	Lennie breaks Curley's wife's
T - 5. CURLEY	E.	What Lennie liked to do to the dead mouse
J - 6. CROOKS	F.	What Lennie wants to tend someday
I - 7. BINDLE	G.	Lennie was accused of this in Weed.
D - 8. NECK	H.	Ranch foreman
K - 9. TRAMP	I.	Slang for a ranch hand's bedroll
H -10. SLIM	J.	Stable man
C -11. FORGOT	K.	Curley's wife acts like one.
O -12. LENNIE	L.	Guy don't need no ___ to be a nice fella
R -13. CARLSON	M.	Lennie carried a dead one in his pocket.
Y -14. HEAVEN	N.	Old swamper whose dog was killed
X -15. FIGHT	O.	He is mentally slow but physically strong.
G -16. RAPE	P.	George's last name
V -17. STEINBECK	Q.	What Slim has that Lennie wants
M -18. MOUSE	R.	Killed Candy's dog
B -19. WEED	S.	Lennie offers to go away and live in one.
U -20. FRIENDS	T.	Ill-tempered son of the ranch owner
E -21. PET	U.	George and Lennie, for example
N -22. CANDY	V.	Author
Q -23. PUPPIES	W.	Place to keep animals and store hay
L -24. SENSE	X.	What Curley likes to do
W -25. BARN	Y.	Nobody gets to ___ and nobody gets no land.

Of Mice and Men Matching 4

___ 1. LENNIE   A. Ill-tempered son of the ranch owner
___ 2. COMPLAIN   B. Lennie offers to go away and live in one.
___ 3. LUGER   C. Killed Candy's dog
___ 4. FORGOT   D. He is mentally slow but physically strong.
___ 5. JAIL   E. I done a ___ thing. I done another ___ thing.
___ 6. SLIM   F. I tell ya a guy gets too lonely an' he gets ___.
___ 7. CARLSON   G. Card game George plays
___ 8. SOLITAIRE   H. Lennie often did this; didn't remember.
___ 9. SENSE   I. Outdoor place ranchers stay overnight
___10. CAMPSITE   J. She's ___ bait all set on the trigger.
___11. PET   K. What Lennie wants to tend someday
___12. RAPE   L. Lennie's aunt who gave him mice
___13. CLARA   M. George had 4 cans of these to eat; Lennie liked ketchup on his
___14. FRIENDS   N. Lennie crushed Curley's
___15. SICK   O. He killed Lennie.
___16. WEED   P. George and Lennie, for example
___17. CURLEY   Q. Town George and Lennie had to leave.
___18. STEINBECK   R. George shot Lennie with it.
___19. MILTON   S. What Lennie liked to do to the dead mouse
___20. BEANS   T. George always ___s about Lennie.
___21. RABBITS   U. Author
___22. CAVE   V. Guy don't need no ___ to be a nice fella
___23. GEORGE   W. Lennie was accused of this in Weed.
___24. BAD   X. George's last name
___25. HAND   Y. Ranch foreman

Of Mice and Men Matching 4 Answer Key

D - 1. LENNIE	A.	Ill-tempered son of the ranch owner
T - 2. COMPLAIN	B.	Lennie offers to go away and live in one.
R - 3. LUGER	C.	Killed Candy's dog
H - 4. FORGOT	D.	He is mentally slow but physically strong.
J - 5. JAIL	E.	I done a ___ thing. I done another ___ thing.
Y - 6. SLIM	F.	I tell ya a guy gets too lonely an' he gets ___.
C - 7. CARLSON	G.	Card game George plays
G - 8. SOLITAIRE	H.	Lennie often did this; didn't remember.
V - 9. SENSE	I.	Outdoor place ranchers stay overnight
I - 10. CAMPSITE	J.	She's ___ bait all set on the trigger.
S - 11. PET	K.	What Lennie wants to tend someday
W - 12. RAPE	L.	Lennie's aunt who gave him mice
L - 13. CLARA	M.	George had 4 cans of these to eat; Lennie liked ketchup on his
P - 14. FRIENDS	N.	Lennie crushed Curley's
F - 15. SICK	O.	He killed Lennie.
Q - 16. WEED	P.	George and Lennie, for example
A - 17. CURLEY	Q.	Town George and Lennie had to leave.
U - 18. STEINBECK	R.	George shot Lennie with it.
X - 19. MILTON	S.	What Lennie liked to do to the dead mouse
M - 20. BEANS	T.	George always ___s about Lennie.
K - 21. RABBITS	U.	Author
B - 22. CAVE	V.	Guy don't need no ___ to be a nice fella
O - 23. GEORGE	W.	Lennie was accused of this in Weed.
E - 24. BAD	X.	George's last name
N - 25. HAND	Y.	Ranch foreman

Of Mice and Men Magic Squares 1

Match the definition with the vocabulary word. Put your answers in the magic squares below. When your answers are correct, all columns and rows will add to the same number.

A. CLARA
B. RAPE
C. CURLEY
D. FORGOT
E. NECK
F. GLOVE
G. CAMPSITE
H. PUPPIES
I. CARLSON
J. COMPLAIN
K. HAND
L. SOLITAIRE
M. CROOKS
N. RABBITS
O. MOUSE
P. BEANS

1. Lennie was accused of this in Weed.
2. Outdoor place ranchers stay overnight
3. Lennie crushed Curley's
4. What Lennie wants to tend someday
5. Stable man
6. Card game George plays
7. What Slim has that Lennie wants
8. Lennie's aunt who gave him mice
9. George had 4 cans of these to eat; Lennie liked ketchup on his
10. Killed Candy's dog
11. Lennie breaks Curley's wife's
12. Lennie often did this; didn't remember.
13. Ill-tempered son of the ranch owner
14. Curley wore one on his left hand.
15. George always ____s about Lennie.
16. Lennie carried a dead one in his pocket.

A=	B=	C=	D=
E=	F=	G=	H=
I=	J=	K=	L=
M=	N=	O=	P=

Of Mice and Men Magic Squares 1 Answer Key

Match the definition with the vocabulary word. Put your answers in the magic squares below. When your answers are correct, all columns and rows will add to the same number.

A. CLARA
B. RAPE
C. CURLEY
D. FORGOT
E. NECK
F. GLOVE
G. CAMPSITE
H. PUPPIES
I. CARLSON
J. COMPLAIN
K. HAND
L. SOLITAIRE
M. CROOKS
N. RABBITS
O. MOUSE
P. BEANS

1. Lennie was accused of this in Weed.
2. Outdoor place ranchers stay overnight
3. Lennie crushed Curley's
4. What Lennie wants to tend someday
5. Stable man
6. Card game George plays
7. What Slim has that Lennie wants
8. Lennie's aunt who gave him mice
9. George had 4 cans of these to eat; Lennie liked ketchup on his
10. Killed Candy's dog
11. Lennie breaks Curley's wife's
12. Lennie often did this; didn't remember.
13. Ill-tempered son of the ranch owner
14. Curley wore one on his left hand.
15. George always ____s about Lennie.
16. Lennie carried a dead one in his pocket.

A=8	B=1	C=13	D=12
E=11	F=14	G=2	H=7
I=10	J=15	K=3	L=6
M=5	N=4	O=16	P=9

Of Mice and Men Magic Squares 2

Match the definition with the vocabulary word. Put your answers in the magic squares below. When your answers are correct, all columns and rows will add to the same number.

A. CAMPSITE E. SICK   I. CLARA   M. CROOKS
B. LENNIE   F. TRAMP   J. NECK   N. MILTON
C. STEINBECK G. GLOVE   K. JAIL   O. BUNK
D. GEORGE   H. BINDLE   L. CURLEY P. LAND

1. Ranch hand's bed
2. He killed Lennie.
3. Lennie breaks Curley's wife's
4. I tell ya a guy gets too lonely an' he gets ___.
5. Lennie's aunt who gave him mice
6. Curley's wife acts like one.
7. What George and Lennie hope to own someday
8. Author

9. Slang for a ranch hand's bedroll
10. She's ___ bait all set on the trigger.
11. Outdoor place ranchers stay overnight
12. George's last name
13. He is mentally slow but physically strong.
14. Stable man
15. Curley wore one on his left hand.
16. Ill-tempered son of the ranch owner

A=	B=	C=	D=
E=	F=	G=	H=
I=	J=	K=	L=
M=	N=	O=	P=

Of Mice and Men Magic Squares 2 Answer Key

Match the definition with the vocabulary word. Put your answers in the magic squares below. When your answers are correct, all columns and rows will add to the same number.

A. CAMPSITE
B. LENNIE
C. STEINBECK
D. GEORGE
E. SICK
F. TRAMP
G. GLOVE
H. BINDLE
I. CLARA
J. NECK
K. JAIL
L. CURLEY
M. CROOKS
N. MILTON
O. BUNK
P. LAND

1. Ranch hand's bed
2. He killed Lennie.
3. Lennie breaks Curley's wife's
4. I tell ya a guy gets too lonely an' he gets ___.
5. Lennie's aunt who gave him mice
6. Curley's wife acts like one.
7. What George and Lennie hope to own someday
8. Author
9. Slang for a ranch hand's bedroll
10. She's ___ bait all set on the trigger.
11. Outdoor place ranchers stay overnight
12. George's last name
13. He is mentally slow but physically strong.
14. Stable man
15. Curley wore one on his left hand.
16. Ill-tempered son of the ranch owner

A=11	B=13	C=8	D=2
E=4	F=6	G=15	H=9
I=5	J=3	K=10	L=16
M=14	N=12	O=1	P=7

24
Copyrighted

Of Mice and Men Magic Squares 3

Match the definition with the vocabulary word. Put your answers in the magic squares below. When your answers are correct, all columns and rows will add to the same number.

A. STEINBECK
B. PUPPIES
C. TRAMP
D. MOUSE
E. SICK
F. SALINAS
G. CARLSON
H. BEANS
I. BINDLE
J. SOLITAIRE
K. SENSE
L. MILTON
M. FUTURE
N. COMPLAIN
O. GLOVE
P. BAD

1. George had 4 cans of these to eat; Lennie liked ketchup on his
2. Author
3. What Slim has that Lennie wants
4. Killed Candy's dog
5. Card game George plays
6. Curley wore one on his left hand.
7. I done a ___ thing. I done another ___ thing.
8. Slang for a ranch hand's bedroll
9. Guy don't need no ___ to be a nice fella
10. George always ___s about Lennie.
11. With us it ain't like that. We got a ___.
12. George's last name
13. I tell ya a guy gets too lonely an' he gets ___.
14. Lennie carried a dead one in his pocket.
15. Curley's wife acts like one.
16. A few miles south of Soledad, this river runs deep and green.

A=	B=	C=	D=
E=	F=	G=	H=
I=	J=	K=	L=
M=	N=	O=	P=

Of Mice and Men Magic Squares 3 Answer Key

Match the definition with the vocabulary word. Put your answers in the magic squares below. When your answers are correct, all columns and rows will add to the same number.

A. STEINBECK   E. SICK   I. BINDLE   M. FUTURE
B. PUPPIES   F. SALINAS   J. SOLITAIRE   N. COMPLAIN
C. TRAMP   G. CARLSON   K. SENSE   O. GLOVE
D. MOUSE   H. BEANS   L. MILTON   P. BAD

1. George had 4 cans of these to eat; Lennie liked ketchup on his
2. Author
3. What Slim has that Lennie wants
4. Killed Candy's dog
5. Card game George plays
6. Curley wore one on his left hand.
7. I done a ___ thing. I done another ___ thing.
8. Slang for a ranch hand's bedroll
9. Guy don't need no ___ to be a nice fella
10. George always ____s about Lennie.
11. With us it ain't like that. We got a ___.
12. George's last name
13. I tell ya a guy gets too lonely an' he gets ___.
14. Lennie carried a dead one in his pocket.
15. Curley's wife acts like one.
16. A few miles south of Soledad, this river runs deep and green.

A=2	B=3	C=15	D=14
E=13	F=16	G=4	H=1
I=8	J=5	K=9	L=12
M=11	N=10	O=6	P=7

Of Mice and Men Magic Squares 4

Match the definition with the vocabulary word. Put your answers in the magic squares below. When your answers are correct, all columns and rows will add to the same number.

A. FIGHT
B. CROOKS
C. JAIL
D. BEANS
E. CAMPSITE
F. LENNIE
G. MILTON
H. BINDLE
I. HEAVEN
J. PET
K. NECK
L. BOSS
M. SICK
N. CLARA
O. HAND
P. LAND

1. I tell ya a guy gets too lonely an' he gets ___.
2. He is mentally slow but physically strong.
3. Slang for a ranch hand's bedroll
4. Lennie crushed Curley's
5. One in charge
6. She's ___ bait all set on the trigger.
7. What Curley likes to do
8. What Lennie liked to do to the dead mouse
9. Lennie breaks Curley's wife's
10. George had 4 cans of these to eat; Lennie liked ketchup on his
11. Stable man
12. Nobody gets to ___ and nobody gets no land.
13. Lennie's aunt who gave him mice
14. Outdoor place ranchers stay overnight
15. George's last name
16. What George and Lennie hope to own someday

A=	B=	C=	D=
E=	F=	G=	H=
I=	J=	K=	L=
M=	N=	O=	P=

27
Copyrighted

Of Mice and Men Magic Squares 4 Answer Key

Match the definition with the vocabulary word. Put your answers in the magic squares below. When your answers are correct, all columns and rows will add to the same number.

A. FIGHT
B. CROOKS
C. JAIL
D. BEANS
E. CAMPSITE
F. LENNIE
G. MILTON
H. BINDLE
I. HEAVEN
J. PET
K. NECK
L. BOSS
M. SICK
N. CLARA
O. HAND
P. LAND

1. I tell ya a guy gets too lonely an' he gets ___.
2. He is mentally slow but physically strong.
3. Slang for a ranch hand's bedroll
4. Lennie crushed Curley's
5. One in charge
6. She's ___ bait all set on the trigger.
7. What Curley likes to do
8. What Lennie liked to do to the dead mouse
9. Lennie breaks Curley's wife's
10. George had 4 cans of these to eat; Lennie liked ketchup on his
11. Stable man
12. Nobody gets to ___ and nobody gets no land.
13. Lennie's aunt who gave him mice
14. Outdoor place ranchers stay overnight
15. George's last name
16. What George and Lennie hope to own someday

A=7	B=11	C=6	D=10
E=14	F=2	G=15	H=3
I=12	J=8	K=9	L=5
M=1	N=13	O=4	P=16

Of Mice and Men Word Search 1

```
L I A J G E O R G E Z N C U R L E Y R D
H A C Q L J S B C M R O T S W K H L A Q
E D N A E Z S N Z A N S K L T C D D B P
A C P D N S W F B Y I L C S I C K B B H
V N L Q N D P I W C A R E L F R P R I S
E F H A I R Y G Q C L A B Q A O P S T S
N N E N Q P H L X P C N L R R T S S D
J B F F D N O T L I M H I D F C A G N M
C F A N B C W B T X O C E D G A W P O G
T C A D V R Y H R W C E T Q N M B B M T
F H J T W O B U N K W W S E I P P U P B
G Q V L K O R S V Q F F S T W S Y P S L
R H S P P K H Q P S R J K Z R I D W O Q
V Y Y P W S F Y Y Z I Z T R N T D T L H
W H R B H A W B Y K E F B X W E B S I K
P L D R M L T G M G N U G S T K I S T H
J P B L Y I B W L X D T T C M L N M A F
B Q L O W N L C K O S U T R A J D A I H
K V M T S A T C H T V R R P A V L L R T
S S K R F S B S E N S E S U O M E L E S
S Y D G L G P N E L G M B H I H P P P S
Z J G J G B X C C U R J L L Z D H N A R
M M F K G S K M L W Y L S S R B G D R R
```

A few miles south of Soledad, this river runs deep and green. (7)
Author (9)
Card game George plays (9)
Curley wore one on his left hand. (5)
Curley's wife acts like one. (5)
George always ____s about Lennie. (8)
George and Lennie, for example (7)
George had 4 cans of these to eat; Lennie liked ketchup on his (5)
George shot Lennie with it. (5)
George's last name (6)
Guy don't need no ____ to be a nice fella (5)
He is mentally slow but physically strong. (6)
He killed Lennie. (6)
I done a ____ thing. I done another ____ thing. (3)
I tell ya a guy gets too lonely an' he gets ____. (4)
Ill-tempered son of the ranch owner (6)
Killed Candy's dog (7)
Lennie breaks Curley's wife's (4)
Lennie carried a dead one in his pocket. (5)
Lennie crushed Curley's (4)
Lennie offers to go away and live in one. (4)
Lennie often did this; didn't remember. (6)

Lennie was accused of this in Weed. (4)
Lennie's aunt who gave him mice (5)
Lennie's last name (5)
Nobody gets to ____ and nobody gets no land. (6)
Old swamper whose dog was killed (5)
One in charge (4)
Outdoor place ranchers stay overnight (8)
Place to keep animals and store hay (4)
Ranch foreman (4)
Ranch hand's bed (4)
She's ____ bait all set on the trigger. (4)
Slang for a ranch hand's bedroll (6)
Stable man (6)
Town George and Lennie had to leave. (4)
What Curley likes to do (5)
What George and Lennie hope to own someday (4)
What Lennie liked to do to the dead mouse (3)
What Lennie wants to tend someday (7)
What Slim has that Lennie wants (7)
With us it ain't like that. We got a ____. (6)

Of Mice and Men Word Search 1 Answer Key

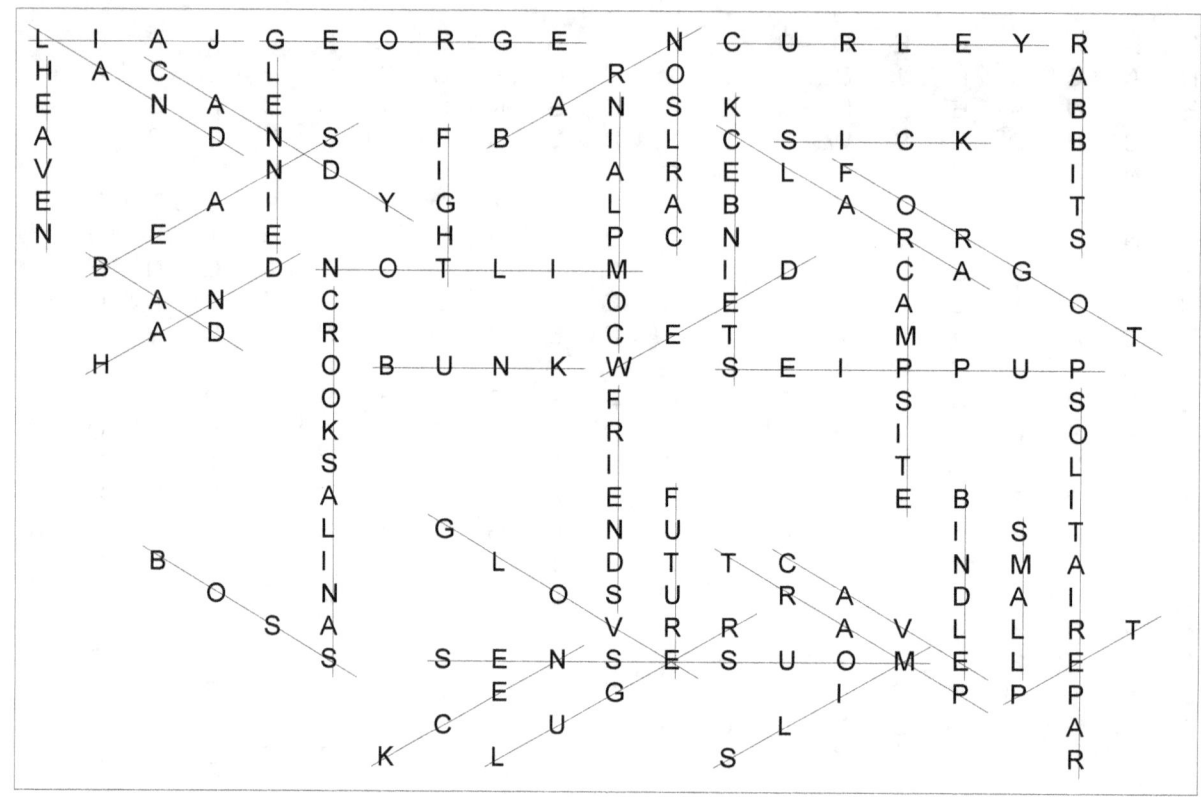

A few miles south of Soledad, this river runs deep and green. (7)
Author (9)
Card game George plays (9)
Curley wore one on his left hand. (5)
Curley's wife acts like one. (5)
George always ____s about Lennie. (8)
George and Lennie, for example (7)
George had 4 cans of these to eat; Lennie liked ketchup on his (5)
George shot Lennie with it. (5)
George's last name (6)
Guy don't need no ___ to be a nice fella (5)
He is mentally slow but physically strong. (6)
He killed Lennie. (6)
I done a ___ thing. I done another ___ thing. (3)
I tell ya a guy gets too lonely an' he gets ___. (4)
Ill-tempered son of the ranch owner (6)
Killed Candy's dog (7)
Lennie breaks Curley's wife's (4)
Lennie carried a dead one in his pocket. (5)
Lennie crushed Curley's (4)
Lennie offers to go away and live in one. (4)
Lennie often did this; didn't remember. (6)

Lennie was accused of this in Weed. (4)
Lennie's aunt who gave him mice (5)
Lennie's last name (5)
Nobody gets to ___ and nobody gets no land. (6)
Old swamper whose dog was killed (5)
One in charge (4)
Outdoor place ranchers stay overnight (8)
Place to keep animals and store hay (4)
Ranch foreman (4)
Ranch hand's bed (4)
She's ___ bait all set on the trigger. (4)
Slang for a ranch hand's bedroll (6)
Stable man (6)
Town George and Lennie had to leave. (4)
What Curley likes to do (5)
What George and Lennie hope to own someday (4)
What Lennie liked to do to the dead mouse (3)
What Lennie wants to tend someday (7)
What Slim has that Lennie wants (7)
With us it ain't like that. We got a ___. (6)

Of Mice and Men Word Search 2

```
C A R L S O N G C R T E W S H W K D C R
X M C H D O V Y E H O V B G M C B B A H
J K L R N X L Z G O G O Y N I A Y F M M
W Y A L E Q G I C V R L K S G G L F P T
D F R B I C F Q T N O G H R R Q X L S F
L J A B R W Z U O A F Q E Z Z P Z Q I F
L G J O F R B T T N I H C J Z X N D T L
W B O Q H J L Y Q U Q R C G B P L Z E R
B K K J F I T F H F R Q E M Q G N D Q L
S L C M M V P Q J C C E J J S V L Z D Y
C D E X M W N F F O K L S P L J D Q L P
X N B T F Z C N H M L L T J C C L F Q J
C W N M J V U W M P M G I B K Y E K V B
G N I R F X R Q Z L Z D B T P L N W W C
G G E C T T L B L A L C B R T W N C A P
R H T S G T E V I I V T A S Z R I V N V
X E S N E S Y L A N D W R R A P E P E M
J O B A B B D M E G D E D A Q R Y U C C
B Y C L L W C V J S G L T X M K V P K Y
J M D A N I A K N U B W E T E P M P K P
A H N R N E N A L J Y A E S T I P I Z R
I L A R H D E A P Y T R D E L P Y E C Q
L B H P R B Y E S U O M D S D C C S C C
```

A few miles south of Soledad, this river runs deep and green. (7)
Author (9)
Card game George plays (9)
Curley wore one on his left hand. (5)
Curley's wife acts like one. (5)
George always ____s about Lennie. (8)
George and Lennie, for example (7)
George had 4 cans of these to eat; Lennie liked ketchup on his (5)
George shot Lennie with it. (5)
George's last name (6)
Guy don't need no ___ to be a nice fella (5)
He is mentally slow but physically strong. (6)
He killed Lennie. (6)
I done a ___ thing. I done another ___ thing. (3)
I tell ya a guy gets too lonely an' he gets ___. (4)
Ill-tempered son of the ranch owner (6)
Killed Candy's dog (7)
Lennie breaks Curley's wife's (4)
Lennie carried a dead one in his pocket. (5)
Lennie crushed Curley's (4)
Lennie offers to go away and live in one. (4)
Lennie often did this; didn't remember. (6)

Lennie was accused of this in Weed. (4)
Lennie's aunt who gave him mice (5)
Lennie's last name (5)
Nobody gets to ___ and nobody gets no land. (6)
Old swamper whose dog was killed (5)
One in charge (4)
Outdoor place ranchers stay overnight (8)
Place to keep animals and store hay (4)
Ranch foreman (4)
Ranch hand's bed (4)
She's ___ bait all set on the trigger. (4)
Slang for a ranch hand's bedroll (6)
Stable man (6)
Town George and Lennie had to leave. (4)
What Curley likes to do (5)
What George and Lennie hope to own someday (4)
What Lennie liked to do to the dead mouse (3)
What Lennie wants to tend someday (7)
What Slim has that Lennie wants (7)
With us it ain't like that. We got a ___. (6)

Of Mice and Men Word Search 2 Answer Key

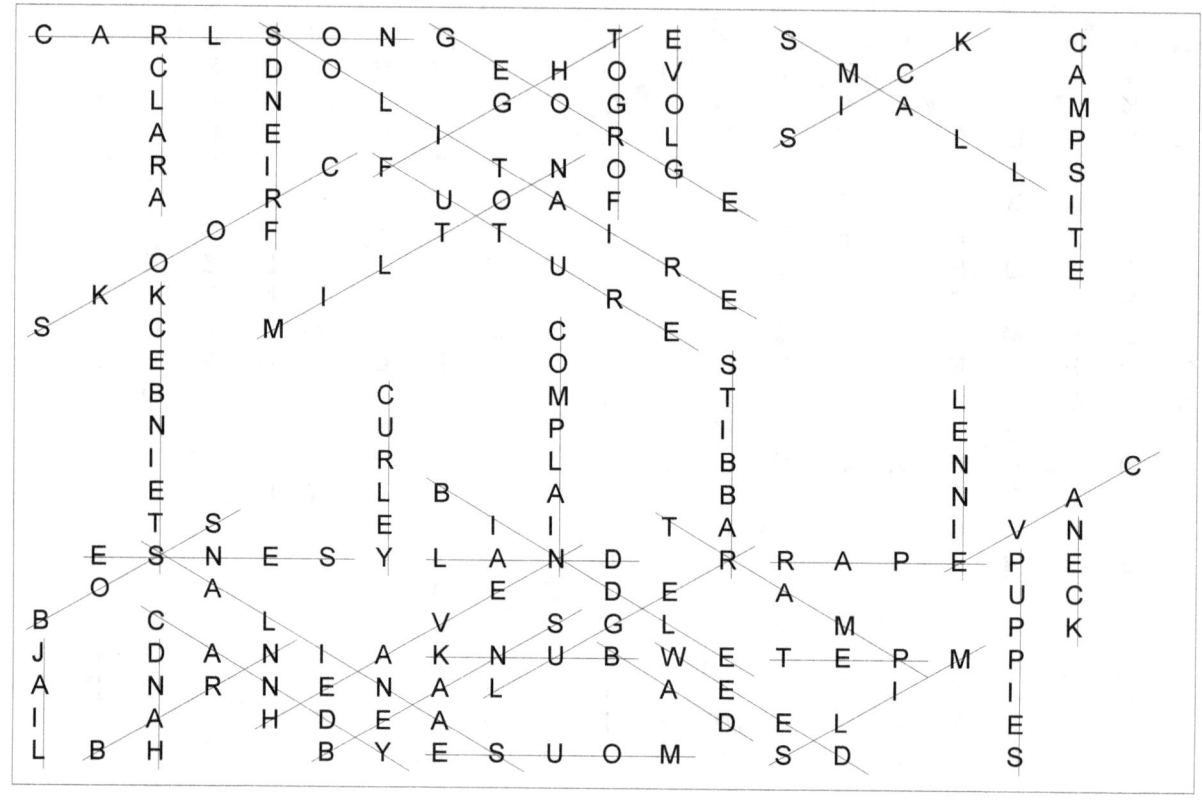

A few miles south of Soledad, this river runs deep and green. (7)
Author (9)
Card game George plays (9)
Curley wore one on his left hand. (5)
Curley's wife acts like one. (5)
George always ____s about Lennie. (8)
George and Lennie, for example (7)
George had 4 cans of these to eat; Lennie liked ketchup on his (5)
George shot Lennie with it. (5)
George's last name (6)
Guy don't need no ___ to be a nice fella (5)
He is mentally slow but physically strong. (6)
He killed Lennie. (6)
I done a ___ thing. I done another ___ thing. (3)
I tell ya a guy gets too lonely an' he gets ___. (4)
Ill-tempered son of the ranch owner (6)
Killed Candy's dog (7)
Lennie breaks Curley's wife's (4)
Lennie carried a dead one in his pocket. (5)
Lennie crushed Curley's (4)
Lennie offers to go away and live in one. (4)
Lennie often did this; didn't remember. (6)

Lennie was accused of this in Weed. (4)
Lennie's aunt who gave him mice (5)
Lennie's last name (5)
Nobody gets to ___ and nobody gets no land. (6)
Old swamper whose dog was killed (5)
One in charge (4)
Outdoor place ranchers stay overnight (8)
Place to keep animals and store hay (4)
Ranch foreman (4)
Ranch hand's bed (4)
She's ___ bait all set on the trigger. (4)
Slang for a ranch hand's bedroll (6)
Stable man (6)
Town George and Lennie had to leave. (4)
What Curley likes to do (5)
What George and Lennie hope to own someday (4)
What Lennie liked to do to the dead mouse (3)
What Lennie wants to tend someday (7)
What Slim has that Lennie wants (7)
With us it ain't like that. We got a ___. (6)

Of Mice and Men Word Search 3

```
H J P S C G H X S K O O R C S L Z Y C K
E W D O S A S S B A X T X R Q F P H K W
A K T L S M R S G M L H F G G B H C S R
V L J I V B D L G S T I B B A R B K K P
E X M T K N H M S Z W D N X V Q X C X N
N D N A E C Q D V O G P J A Y N E C V F
F M V I W L C D N C N M H C S B Y Y N Q
P X R R N C Q W K M S Z J H N S D S N S
C F P E L H D X T H P W B I F S D W F F
M X E Q V R P H G G Q B E Z P V N B L V
J D T X S X D J C W S T I V X I X B B C
B J I L F J C Q K N S R N N A S B P L R
D F S M S A B M C H D X N L D M B P A J
M L P R I I P O I Y F X P B Y L G P N Y
V S M A L L N E S U O M C U R L E Y D G
W G A K U C T E Y S O R D P O R N N N M
Z K C G X B I O X C H W F V U T A S A M
Z E E X A P L F N P Y N E T L C B E H W
N R F R P M Q O G G R X U E B E A N S X
M X A U R A G R S A B F N P G U Y S D Y
F L P Z Y R S G B L R N B K T Y N E Q R
C F I G H T C O G A I C A V E R E K C K
V G E O R G E T Z E D M Y B M W R T S M
```

BAD	CAVE	GEORGE	MOUSE	SLIM
BARN	CLARA	GLOVE	NECK	SMALL
BEANS	COMPLAIN	HAND	PET	SOLITAIRE
BINDLE	CROOKS	HEAVEN	PUPPIES	STEINBECK
BOSS	CURLEY	JAIL	RABBITS	TRAMP
BUNK	FIGHT	LAND	RAPE	WEED
CAMPSITE	FORGOT	LENNIE	SALINAS	
CANDY	FRIENDS	LUGER	SENSE	
CARLSON	FUTURE	MILTON	SICK	

Of Mice and Men Word Search 3 Answer Key

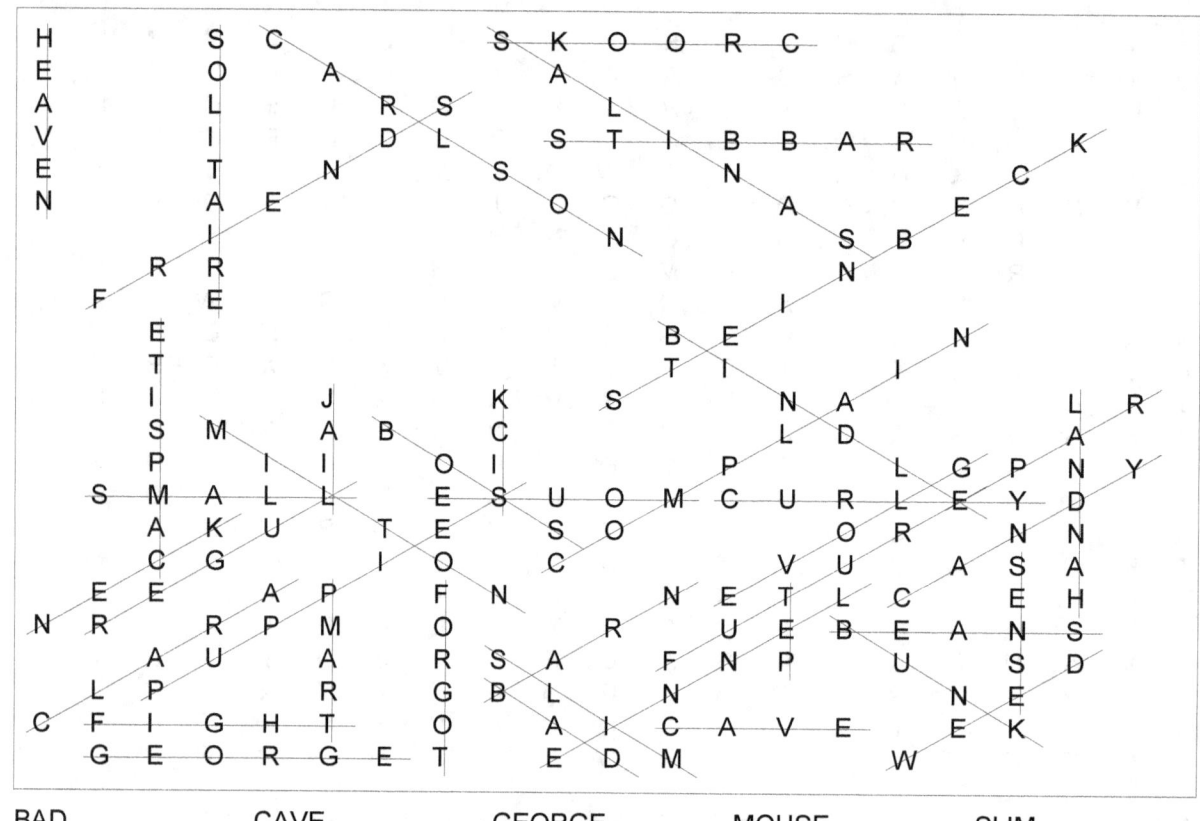

BAD	CAVE	GEORGE	MOUSE	SLIM
BARN	CLARA	GLOVE	NECK	SMALL
BEANS	COMPLAIN	HAND	PET	SOLITAIRE
BINDLE	CROOKS	HEAVEN	PUPPIES	STEINBECK
BOSS	CURLEY	JAIL	RABBITS	TRAMP
BUNK	FIGHT	LAND	RAPE	WEED
CAMPSITE	FORGOT	LENNIE	SALINAS	
CANDY	FRIENDS	LUGER	SENSE	
CARLSON	FUTURE	MILTON	SICK	

Of Mice and Men Word Search 4

```
N K Q D J C X W G Q X J W G L C X M J B
N D T R C G P X N B D T F K M W M P L Z P
G M Z C T F Q G P S R M H P B J T L M P Z
M T K K C H C M R Y M C M B B P B T G M G
G S N K B M A Q M H C R X M W M R S S Z Z
S C M F M I R P M G Z V B G F C L K Q Z Z
N E W H O L Y N L G Z D M I Z H O N P
H C N C U T S C X O S E P H G S J O E N
B A C S S O O K L V R J O E H S N R C K W
B I N L E N I E E P M A R T S I C K F F
S A N D S U P R G B I N A I G Z Q O F W
T L D D B V U H L W P B A L E Z M G Y
E S P W L T L F S B E B Z T P T K P Z M
I G U K U E H S S A A J D I D I R L W M N
N K P F C R E L P R M N E L R S V A L L T
B Y P C G H A V D N A S E O W P D I G L T
E C I A P Q V Y S L C Q W S L M Z N L G S
C L E V Z G E D M Y B C L A R A B O S D
K A S E B B N Z E B T E M L S C T D P D Y
X G N G G E W L K K D V A I P M N X W Y
Q S T D I M R F O R G O T N N W A T H Y
R X T R Y U K B W D C R Y A S B M L D R J
Q X F K C R J F K X V R M S Q P F W L J
```

BAD	CAVE	GEORGE	MOUSE	SLIM
BARN	CLARA	GLOVE	NECK	SMALL
BEANS	COMPLAIN	HAND	PET	SOLITAIRE
BINDLE	CROOKS	HEAVEN	PUPPIES	STEINBECK
BOSS	CURLEY	JAIL	RABBITS	TRAMP
BUNK	FIGHT	LAND	RAPE	WEED
CAMPSITE	FORGOT	LENNIE	SALINAS	
CANDY	FRIENDS	LUGER	SENSE	
CARLSON	FUTURE	MILTON	SICK	

Of Mice and Men Word Search 4 Answer Key

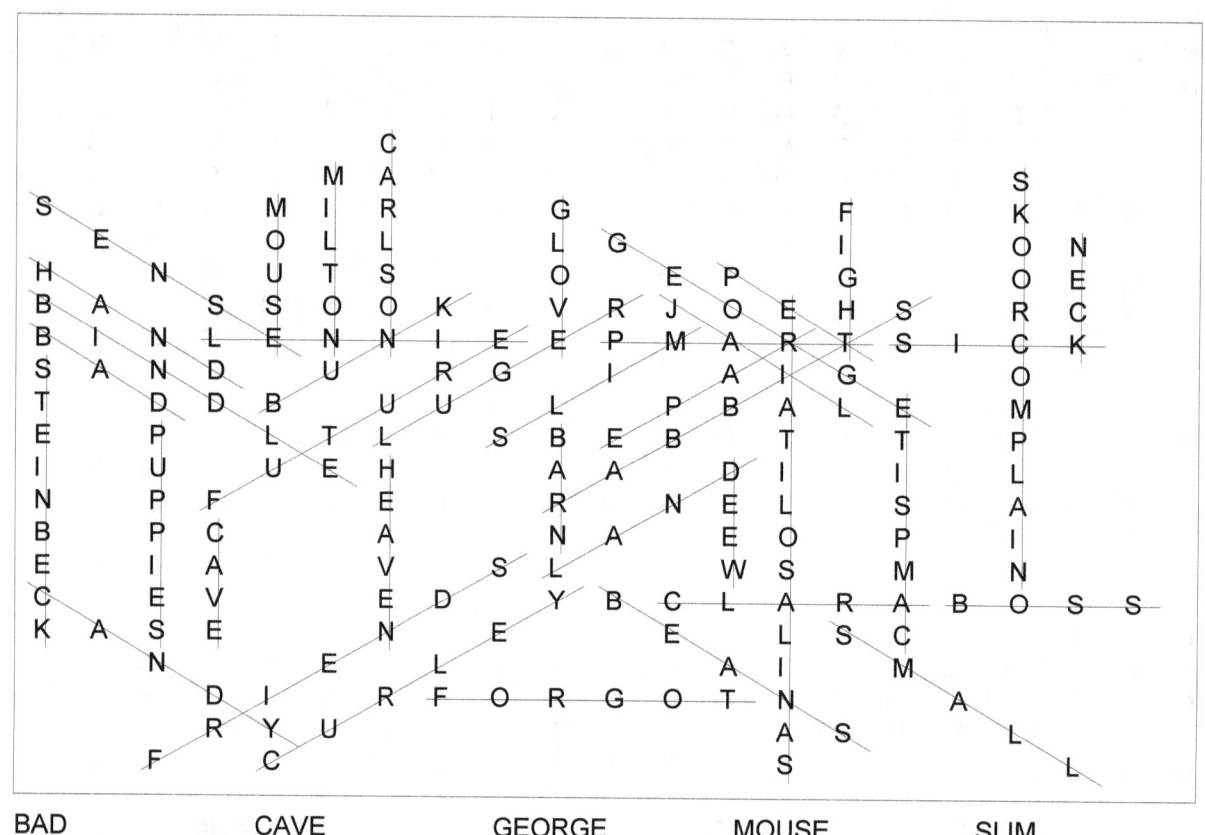

BAD	CAVE	GEORGE	MOUSE	SLIM
BARN	CLARA	GLOVE	NECK	SMALL
BEANS	COMPLAIN	HAND	PET	SOLITAIRE
BINDLE	CROOKS	HEAVEN	PUPPIES	STEINBECK
BOSS	CURLEY	JAIL	RABBITS	TRAMP
BUNK	FIGHT	LAND	RAPE	WEED
CAMPSITE	FORGOT	LENNIE	SALINAS	
CANDY	FRIENDS	LUGER	SENSE	
CARLSON	FUTURE	MILTON	SICK	

Of Mice and Men Crossword 1

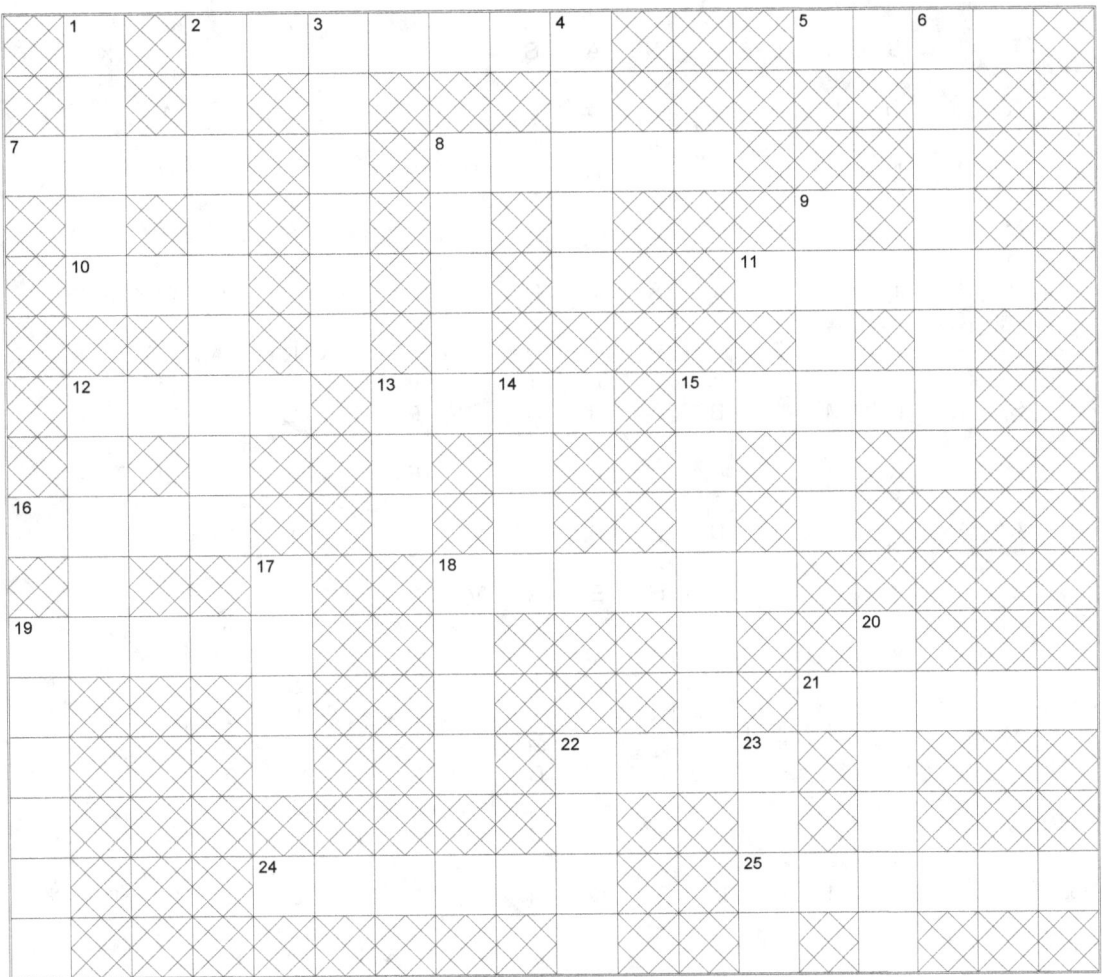

Across
2. A few miles south of Soledad, this river runs deep and green.
5. Lennie breaks Curley's wife's
7. She's ___ bait all set on the trigger.
8. Old swamper whose dog was killed
10. What Lennie liked to do to the dead mouse
11. Lennie carried a dead one in his pocket.
12. Ranch foreman
13. Place to keep animals and store hay
15. What Curley likes to do
16. Lennie offers to go away and live in one.
18. Nobody gets to ___ and nobody gets no land.
19. Curley wore one on his left hand.
21. George shot Lennie with it.
22. One in charge
24. George's last name
25. Ill-tempered son of the ranch owner

Down
1. Curley's wife acts like one.
2. Card game George plays
3. He is mentally slow but physically strong.
4. Guy don't need no ___ to be a nice fella
6. Outdoor place ranchers stay overnight
8. Lennie's aunt who gave him mice
9. Lennie often did this; didn't remember.
12. Lennie's last name
13. I done a ___ thing. I done another ___ thing.
14. Lennie was accused of this in Weed.
15. George and Lennie, for example
17. Town George and Lennie had to leave.
18. Lennie crushed Curley's
19. He killed Lennie.
20. With us it ain't like that. We got a ___.
22. Ranch hand's bed
23. I tell ya a guy gets too lonely an' he gets ___.

Of Mice and Men Crossword 1 Answer Key

	1 T	2 S	A	3 L	I	N	4 A	S		5 N	6 E	C	K
	R	O		E			E				A		
7 J	A	I	L			8 C	A	N	D	Y		M	
	M	I		N		L		S		9 F		P	
10 P	E	T		I		A		E		11 M	O	U	S	E
		A		E		R				R		I	
	12 S	L	I	M		13 B	14 A	R	N	15 F	I	G	H	T
	M		R			A		A		R		O		E
16 C	A	V	E			D		P		I		T	
	L		17 W		18 H	E	A	V	E	N			
19 G	L	O	V	E		A				N		20 F	
E			E			N				D		21 L	U	G	E	R
O			D			D		22 B	O	23 S		T	
R								U		I		U	
G			24 M	I	L	T	O	N		25 C	U	R	L	E	Y
E								K		K		E	

Across
2. A few miles south of Soledad, this river runs deep and green.
5. Lennie breaks Curley's wife's
7. She's ___ bait all set on the trigger.
8. Old swamper whose dog was killed
10. What Lennie liked to do to the dead mouse
11. Lennie carried a dead one in his pocket.
12. Ranch foreman
13. Place to keep animals and store hay
15. What Curley likes to do
16. Lennie offers to go away and live in one.
18. Nobody gets to ___ and nobody gets no land.
19. Curley wore one on his left hand.
21. George shot Lennie with it.
22. One in charge
24. George's last name
25. Ill-tempered son of the ranch owner

Down
1. Curley's wife acts like one.
2. Card game George plays
3. He is mentally slow but physically strong.
4. Guy don't need no ___ to be a nice fella
6. Outdoor place ranchers stay overnight
8. Lennie's aunt who gave him mice
9. Lennie often did this; didn't remember.
12. Lennie's last name
13. I done a ___ thing. I done another ___ thing.
14. Lennie was accused of this in Weed.
15. George and Lennie, for example
17. Town George and Lennie had to leave.
18. Lennie crushed Curley's
19. He killed Lennie.
20. With us it ain't like that. We got a ___.
22. Ranch hand's bed
23. I tell ya a guy gets too lonely an' he gets ___.

Of Mice and Men Crossword 2

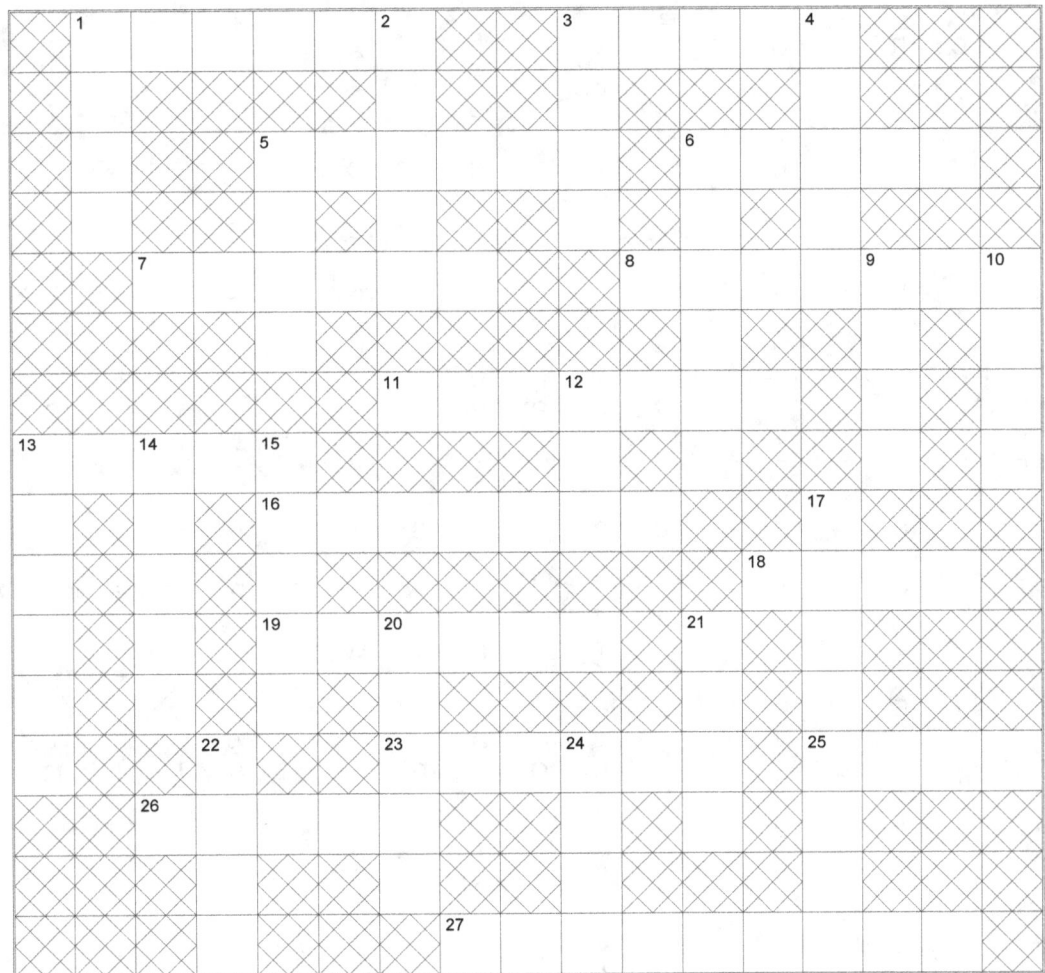

Across
1. Stable man
3. George had 4 cans of these to eat; Lennie liked ketchup on his
5. Nobody gets to ___ and nobody gets no land.
6. Old swamper whose dog was killed
7. Slang for a ranch hand's bedroll
8. George and Lennie, for example
11. What Slim has that Lennie wants
13. What Curley likes to do
16. What Lennie wants to tend someday
18. Place to keep animals and store hay
19. George's last name
23. He killed Lennie.
25. Ranch foreman
26. Lennie carried a dead one in his pocket.
27. Author

Down
1. Lennie offers to go away and live in one.
2. Lennie's last name
3. Ranch hand's bed
4. Guy don't need no ___ to be a nice fella
5. Lennie crushed Curley's
6. Ill-tempered son of the ranch owner
9. Lennie breaks Curley's wife's
10. I tell ya a guy gets too lonely an' he gets ___.
12. What Lennie liked to do to the dead mouse
13. With us it ain't like that. We got a ___.
14. Curley wore one on his left hand.
15. Curley's wife acts like one.
17. Outdoor place ranchers stay overnight
20. George shot Lennie with it.
21. Town George and Lennie had to leave.
22. One in charge
24. Lennie was accused of this in Weed.

Of Mice and Men Crossword 2 Answer Key

Across
1. Stable man
3. George had 4 cans of these to eat; Lennie liked ketchup on his
5. Nobody gets to ___ and nobody gets no land.
6. Old swamper whose dog was killed
7. Slang for a ranch hand's bedroll
8. George and Lennie, for example
11. What Slim has that Lennie wants
13. What Curley likes to do
16. What Lennie wants to tend someday
18. Place to keep animals and store hay
19. George's last name
23. He killed Lennie.
25. Ranch foreman
26. Lennie carried a dead one in his pocket.
27. Author

Down
1. Lennie offers to go away and live in one.
2. Lennie's last name
3. Ranch hand's bed
4. Guy don't need no ___ to be a nice fella
5. Lennie crushed Curley's
6. Ill-tempered son of the ranch owner
9. Lennie breaks Curley's wife's
10. I tell ya a guy gets too lonely an' he gets ___.
12. What Lennie liked to do to the dead mouse
13. With us it ain't like that. We got a ___.
14. Curley wore one on his left hand.
15. Curley's wife acts like one.
17. Outdoor place ranchers stay overnight
20. George shot Lennie with it.
21. Town George and Lennie had to leave.
22. One in charge
24. Lennie was accused of this in Weed.

Of Mice and Men Crossword 3

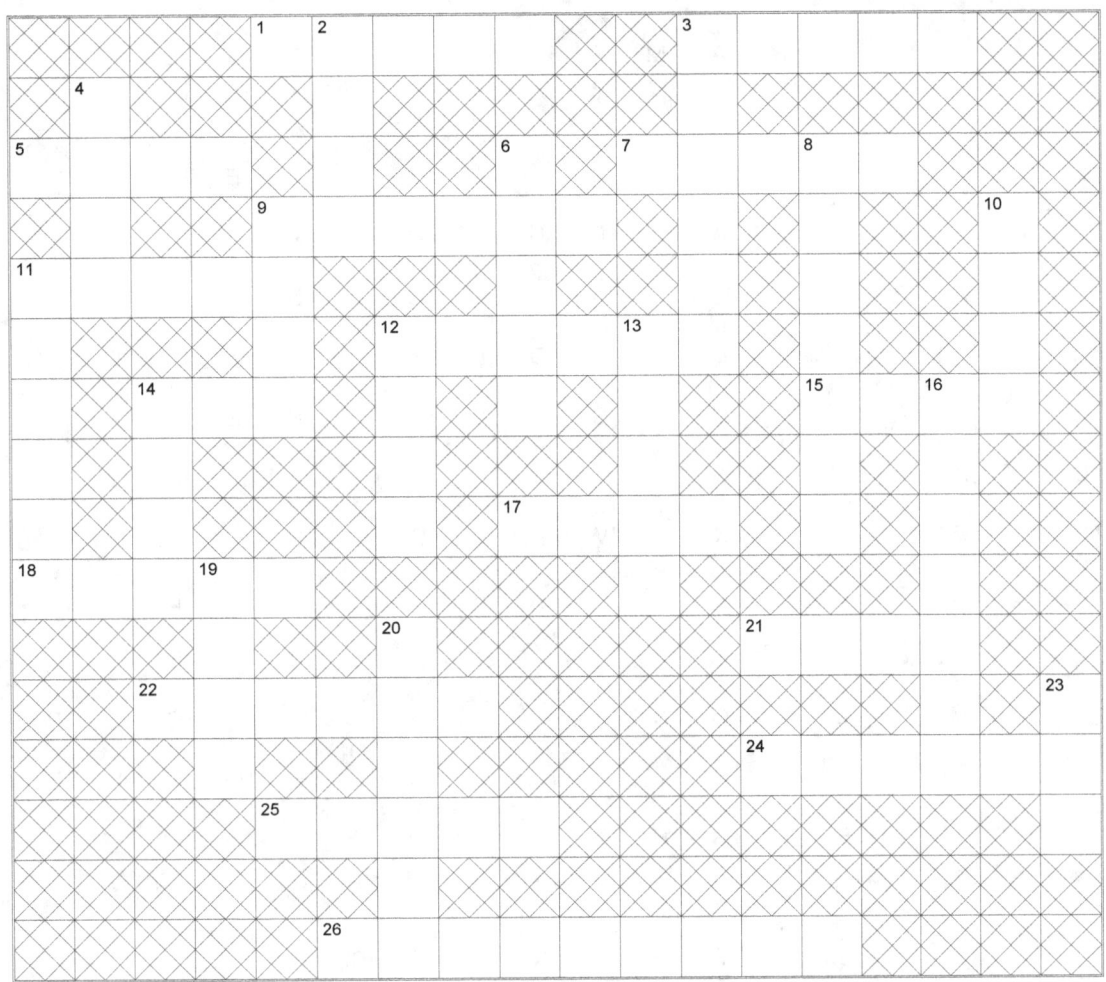

Across
1. Curley's wife acts like one.
3. Curley wore one on his left hand.
5. What George and Lennie hope to own someday
7. Lennie carried a dead one in his pocket.
9. Nobody gets to ___ and nobody gets no land.
11. Lennie's aunt who gave him mice
12. Slang for a ranch hand's bedroll
14. I done a ___ thing. I done another ___ thing.
15. Lennie breaks Curley's wife's
17. Town George and Lennie had to leave.
18. Guy don't need no ___ to be a nice fella
21. One in charge
22. George's last name
24. He is mentally slow but physically strong.
25. What Curley likes to do
26. Author

Down
2. Lennie was accused of this in Weed.
3. He killed Lennie.
4. She's ___ bait all set on the trigger.
6. George had 4 cans of these to eat; Lennie liked ketchup on his
8. A few miles south of Soledad, this river runs deep and green.
9. Lennie crushed Curley's
10. I tell ya a guy gets too lonely an' he gets ___.
11. Stable man
12. Ranch hand's bed
13. George shot Lennie with it.
14. Place to keep animals and store hay
16. Killed Candy's dog
19. Ranch foreman
20. Lennie often did this; didn't remember.
23. What Lennie liked to do to the dead mouse

Of Mice and Men Crossword 3 Answer Key

			¹T	²R	A	M	P		³G	L	O	V	E	
	⁴J			A					E					
⁵L	A	N	D		P		⁶B		⁷M	O	U	⁸S	E	
	I			⁹H	E	A	V	E	N		R		A		¹⁰S
¹¹C	L	A	R	A			A				G		L		I
R				N		¹²B	I	N	D	¹³L	E		I		C
O	¹⁴B	A	D			U		S		U		¹⁵N	¹⁶E	C	K
O	A					N				G		A		A	
K	R				¹⁷W	K	E	E	D			S		R	
¹⁸S	E	N	¹⁹S	E					R				L		
			L		²⁰F						²¹B	O	S	S	
	²²M	I	L	T	O	N							O		²³P
			M		R					²⁴L	E	N	N	I	E
		²⁵F	I	G	H	T									T
					O										
		²⁶S	T	E	I	N	B	E	C	K					

Across
1. Curley's wife acts like one.
3. Curley wore one on his left hand.
5. What George and Lennie hope to own someday
7. Lennie carried a dead one in his pocket.
9. Nobody gets to ___ and nobody gets no land.
11. Lennie's aunt who gave him mice
12. Slang for a ranch hand's bedroll
14. I done a ___ thing. I done another ___ thing.
15. Lennie breaks Curley's wife's
17. Town George and Lennie had to leave.
18. Guy don't need no ___ to be a nice fella
21. One in charge
22. George's last name
24. He is mentally slow but physically strong.
25. What Curley likes to do
26. Author

Down
2. Lennie was accused of this in Weed.
3. He killed Lennie.
4. She's ___ bait all set on the trigger.
6. George had 4 cans of these to eat; Lennie liked ketchup on his
8. A few miles south of Soledad, this river runs deep and green.
9. Lennie crushed Curley's
10. I tell ya a guy gets too lonely an' he gets ___.
11. Stable man
12. Ranch hand's bed
13. George shot Lennie with it.
14. Place to keep animals and store hay
16. Killed Candy's dog
19. Ranch foreman
20. Lennie often did this; didn't remember.
23. What Lennie liked to do to the dead mouse

Of Mice and Men Crossword 4

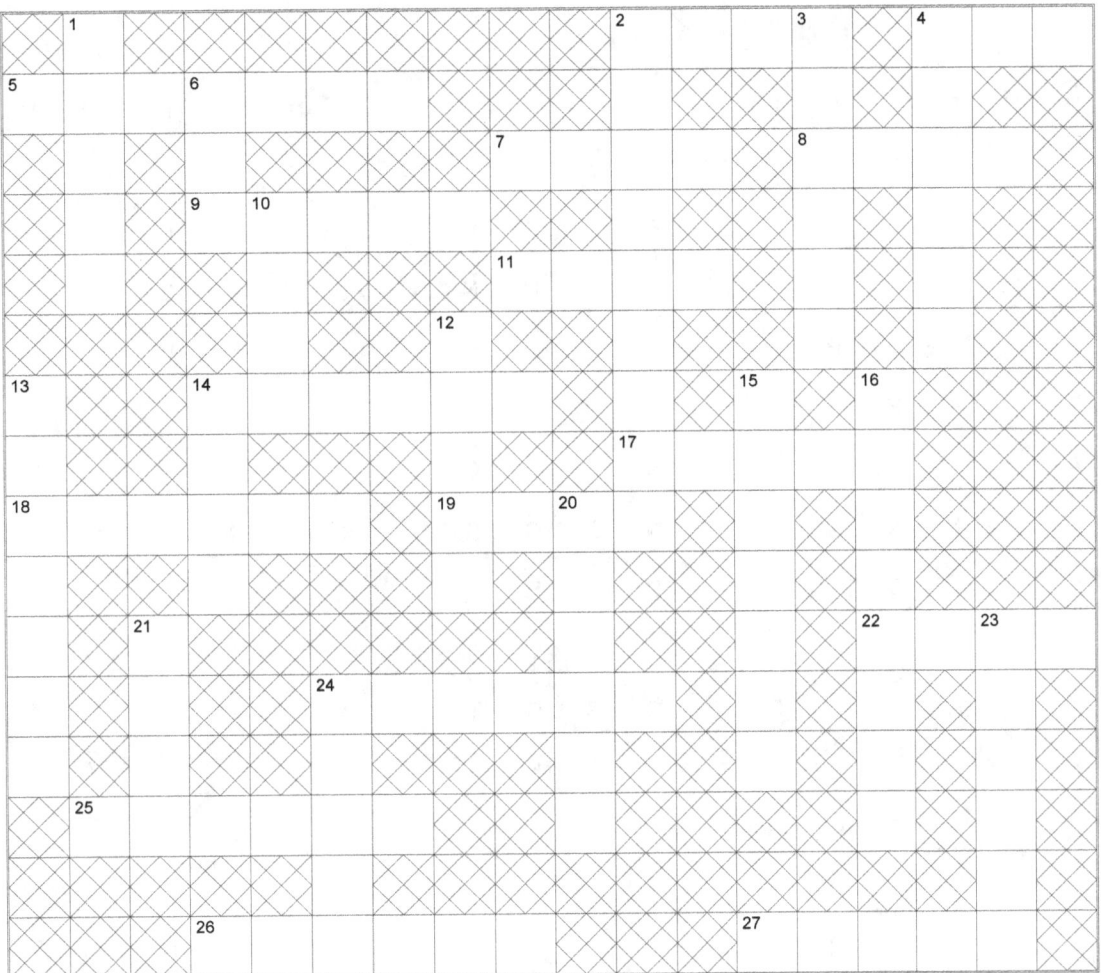

Across
2. Ranch foreman
4. I done a ___ thing. I done another ___ thing.
5. What Slim has that Lennie wants
7. Town George and Lennie had to leave.
8. What George and Lennie hope to own someday
9. Curley's wife acts like one.
11. Ranch hand's bed
14. Nobody gets to ___ and nobody gets no land.
17. Lennie's aunt who gave him mice
18. He is mentally slow but physically strong.
19. Lennie breaks Curley's wife's
22. I tell ya a guy gets too lonely an' he gets ___.
24. Lennie often did this; didn't remember.
25. He killed Lennie.
26. With us it ain't like that. We got a ___.
27. Old swamper whose dog was killed

Down
1. George shot Lennie with it.
2. Author
3. George's last name
4. Slang for a ranch hand's bedroll
6. What Lennie liked to do to the dead mouse
10. Lennie was accused of this in Weed.
12. George had 4 cans of these to eat; Lennie liked ketchup on his
13. A few miles south of Soledad, this river runs deep and green.
14. Lennie crushed Curley's
15. Killed Candy's dog
16. Outdoor place ranchers stay overnight
20. Stable man
21. Lennie offers to go away and live in one.
23. Ill-tempered son of the ranch owner
24. What Curley likes to do

Of Mice and Men Crossword 4 Answer Key

		1 L						2 S	L	3 M		4 B	A	D
5 P	U	P	P	6 I	E	S		T		I		I		
		G		E			7 W	E	E	D	8 L	A	N	D
		E		9 T	10 R	A	M	P			T		D	
		R			A			11 B	U	N	K	O	L	
					P		12 B		B			N		E
13 S		14 H	E	A	V	E	N		E		15 C		16 C	
A		A			A			17 C	L	A	R	A		
18 L	E	N	N	I	E		19 N	E	20 C	K		R		M
I		D			S			R			L		P	
N		21 C						O			S		22 S	I	23 C	K
A		A		24 F	O	R	G	O	T		O		I		U
S		V		I				K			N		T		R
		25 G	E	O	R	G	E		S			E		L
				H										E
				26 F	U	T	U	R	E		27 C	A	N	D	Y

Across
2. Ranch foreman
4. I done a ___ thing. I done another ___ thing.
5. What Slim has that Lennie wants
7. Town George and Lennie had to leave.
8. What George and Lennie hope to own someday
9. Curley's wife acts like one.
11. Ranch hand's bed
14. Nobody gets to ___ and nobody gets no land.
17. Lennie's aunt who gave him mice
18. He is mentally slow but physically strong.
19. Lennie breaks Curley's wife's
22. I tell ya a guy gets too lonely an' he gets ___.
24. Lennie often did this; didn't remember.
25. He killed Lennie.
26. With us it ain't like that. We got a ___.
27. Old swamper whose dog was killed

Down
1. George shot Lennie with it.
2. Author
3. George's last name
4. Slang for a ranch hand's bedroll
6. What Lennie liked to do to the dead mouse
10. Lennie was accused of this in Weed.
12. George had 4 cans of these to eat; Lennie liked ketchup on his
13. A few miles south of Soledad, this river runs deep and green.
14. Lennie crushed Curley's
15. Killed Candy's dog
16. Outdoor place ranchers stay overnight
20. Stable man
21. Lennie offers to go away and live in one.
23. Ill-tempered son of the ranch owner
24. What Curley likes to do

Of Mice and Men

GEORGE	BAD	FORGOT	CURLEY	HAND
RABBITS	RAPE	BEANS	SLIM	BUNK
WEED	CANDY	FREE SPACE	BINDLE	CLARA
STEINBECK	FUTURE	MOUSE	SALINAS	NECK
FRIENDS	CAVE	PET	TRAMP	MILTON

Of Mice and Men

CAMPSITE	COMPLAIN	GLOVE	BARN	PUPPIES
JAIL	SENSE	LENNIE	SOLITAIRE	SICK
LUGER	LAND	FREE SPACE	CARLSON	SMALL
FIGHT	HEAVEN	MILTON	TRAMP	PET
CAVE	FRIENDS	NECK	SALINAS	MOUSE

Of Mice and Men

FORGOT	JAIL	COMPLAIN	LAND	GEORGE
FRIENDS	CARLSON	PET	BARN	BUNK
BINDLE	MOUSE	FREE SPACE	GLOVE	RAPE
SOLITAIRE	STEINBECK	CAMPSITE	CAVE	BEANS
SMALL	LUGER	HAND	RABBITS	FIGHT

Of Mice and Men

NECK	BOSS	LENNIE	MILTON	SENSE
BAD	PUPPIES	HEAVEN	WEED	CANDY
SICK	TRAMP	FREE SPACE	SLIM	SALINAS
FUTURE	CROOKS	FIGHT	RABBITS	HAND
LUGER	SMALL	BEANS	CAVE	CAMPSITE

Of Mice and Men

HAND	BOSS	MOUSE	BARN	CLARA
RABBITS	SENSE	CAVE	JAIL	BINDLE
CANDY	FORGOT	FREE SPACE	PET	SICK
GEORGE	HEAVEN	MILTON	SLIM	CARLSON
SMALL	CURLEY	COMPLAIN	PUPPIES	BAD

Of Mice and Men

NECK	RAPE	WEED	BEANS	CAMPSITE
LUGER	TRAMP	CROOKS	GLOVE	FUTURE
FIGHT	LAND	FREE SPACE	SOLITAIRE	FRIENDS
LENNIE	SALINAS	BAD	PUPPIES	COMPLAIN
CURLEY	SMALL	CARLSON	SLIM	MILTON

Of Mice and Men

CLARA	HAND	LAND	BOSS	SOLITAIRE
BUNK	FRIENDS	SLIM	PUPPIES	RABBITS
CAMPSITE	WEED	FREE SPACE	FUTURE	LUGER
TRAMP	BINDLE	CROOKS	COMPLAIN	RAPE
CANDY	FIGHT	STEINBECK	CARLSON	NECK

Of Mice and Men

HEAVEN	GEORGE	JAIL	MOUSE	PET
FORGOT	BAD	CURLEY	CAVE	BARN
LENNIE	SICK	FREE SPACE	SMALL	MILTON
SENSE	BEANS	NECK	CARLSON	STEINBECK
FIGHT	CANDY	RAPE	COMPLAIN	CROOKS

Of Mice and Men

FUTURE	CURLEY	LENNIE	CROOKS	STEINBECK
CLARA	SICK	LAND	RABBITS	LUGER
SOLITAIRE	SMALL	FREE SPACE	HEAVEN	PET
MOUSE	CAVE	CARLSON	BOSS	GLOVE
NECK	JAIL	GEORGE	BINDLE	HAND

Of Mice and Men

COMPLAIN	MILTON	FIGHT	SENSE	PUPPIES
CANDY	BEANS	RAPE	CAMPSITE	FORGOT
BARN	SALINAS	FREE SPACE	SLIM	TRAMP
WEED	BAD	HAND	BINDLE	GEORGE
JAIL	NECK	GLOVE	BOSS	CARLSON

Of Mice and Men

PET	FORGOT	BINDLE	BAD	BEANS
COMPLAIN	CURLEY	STEINBECK	MILTON	PUPPIES
FIGHT	SMALL	FREE SPACE	BARN	SALINAS
SLIM	TRAMP	LUGER	SICK	CAVE
HAND	HEAVEN	FUTURE	CLARA	CAMPSITE

Of Mice and Men

CANDY	MOUSE	LAND	BUNK	NECK
WEED	SENSE	RABBITS	RAPE	BOSS
JAIL	GLOVE	FREE SPACE	FRIENDS	CROOKS
LENNIE	CARLSON	CAMPSITE	CLARA	FUTURE
HEAVEN	HAND	CAVE	SICK	LUGER

Of Mice and Men

HAND	BAD	BUNK	MOUSE	RABBITS
SOLITAIRE	LENNIE	GEORGE	SMALL	FORGOT
SLIM	RAPE	FREE SPACE	NECK	MILTON
BOSS	JAIL	PET	BINDLE	CARLSON
FRIENDS	STEINBECK	CLARA	WEED	TRAMP

Of Mice and Men

CURLEY	CROOKS	HEAVEN	BARN	FUTURE
BEANS	SICK	COMPLAIN	LAND	SALINAS
FIGHT	CAMPSITE	FREE SPACE	CANDY	GLOVE
SENSE	PUPPIES	TRAMP	WEED	CLARA
STEINBECK	FRIENDS	CARLSON	BINDLE	PET

Of Mice and Men

SOLITAIRE	BINDLE	NECK	SALINAS	SENSE
MOUSE	MILTON	BUNK	SICK	CLARA
FRIENDS	LENNIE	FREE SPACE	BAD	BOSS
CAMPSITE	JAIL	CANDY	FORGOT	CURLEY
HAND	CAVE	FUTURE	CARLSON	PET

Of Mice and Men

LAND	BARN	FIGHT	CROOKS	COMPLAIN
WEED	STEINBECK	SMALL	HEAVEN	RABBITS
LUGER	RAPE	FREE SPACE	GEORGE	GLOVE
BEANS	PUPPIES	PET	CARLSON	FUTURE
CAVE	HAND	CURLEY	FORGOT	CANDY

Of Mice and Men

FRIENDS	CROOKS	CAMPSITE	RABBITS	CANDY
HEAVEN	BEANS	LENNIE	CAVE	SICK
PET	NECK	FREE SPACE	SLIM	BAD
STEINBECK	GLOVE	BARN	LAND	CURLEY
SOLITAIRE	WEED	LUGER	TRAMP	GEORGE

Of Mice and Men

SALINAS	BINDLE	JAIL	SMALL	SENSE
FIGHT	BOSS	RAPE	BUNK	COMPLAIN
HAND	CARLSON	FREE SPACE	FORGOT	FUTURE
MILTON	PUPPIES	GEORGE	TRAMP	LUGER
WEED	SOLITAIRE	CURLEY	LAND	BARN

Of Mice and Men

BEANS	BARN	FORGOT	BINDLE	SENSE
BAD	SOLITAIRE	LENNIE	GLOVE	COMPLAIN
JAIL	FUTURE	FREE SPACE	MOUSE	HEAVEN
CROOKS	SICK	BUNK	WEED	SLIM
HAND	RABBITS	SALINAS	CLARA	LUGER

Of Mice and Men

CAVE	STEINBECK	PUPPIES	RAPE	CANDY
NECK	TRAMP	CURLEY	MILTON	CARLSON
SMALL	BOSS	FREE SPACE	CAMPSITE	FRIENDS
PET	LAND	LUGER	CLARA	SALINAS
RABBITS	HAND	SLIM	WEED	BUNK

Of Mice and Men

SENSE	FUTURE	LENNIE	HAND	CARLSON
SICK	GLOVE	COMPLAIN	TRAMP	SMALL
HEAVEN	SALINAS	FREE SPACE	SLIM	BAD
PUPPIES	FIGHT	WEED	MOUSE	LUGER
JAIL	STEINBECK	PET	BUNK	MILTON

Of Mice and Men

CROOKS	NECK	RAPE	BEANS	BINDLE
BARN	CAVE	FRIENDS	GEORGE	CURLEY
CLARA	CAMPSITE	FREE SPACE	CANDY	RABBITS
FORGOT	LAND	MILTON	BUNK	PET
STEINBECK	JAIL	LUGER	MOUSE	WEED

Of Mice and Men

CAVE	SOLITAIRE	RAPE	LAND	LENNIE
FORGOT	FRIENDS	GLOVE	SICK	FUTURE
STEINBECK	RABBITS	FREE SPACE	BOSS	FIGHT
GEORGE	LUGER	CURLEY	SMALL	CARLSON
CANDY	BINDLE	BUNK	TRAMP	BAD

Of Mice and Men

SENSE	SALINAS	CAMPSITE	SLIM	CROOKS
PUPPIES	MOUSE	COMPLAIN	PET	CLARA
HEAVEN	HAND	FREE SPACE	MILTON	BEANS
NECK	JAIL	BAD	TRAMP	BUNK
BINDLE	CANDY	CARLSON	SMALL	CURLEY

Of Mice and Men

MILTON	GLOVE	HAND	CLARA	BEANS
MOUSE	GEORGE	CAMPSITE	FRIENDS	SENSE
SICK	CURLEY	FREE SPACE	BARN	HEAVEN
COMPLAIN	FORGOT	CROOKS	SOLITAIRE	BINDLE
WEED	LAND	LENNIE	CARLSON	BAD

Of Mice and Men

FIGHT	LUGER	STEINBECK	RABBITS	PUPPIES
CAVE	TRAMP	SALINAS	RAPE	PET
JAIL	FUTURE	FREE SPACE	BUNK	SMALL
SLIM	CANDY	BAD	CARLSON	LENNIE
LAND	WEED	BINDLE	SOLITAIRE	CROOKS

Of Mice and Men

RABBITS	BOSS	BARN	CROOKS	CLARA
JAIL	STEINBECK	PUPPIES	MOUSE	BINDLE
CAMPSITE	RAPE	FREE SPACE	FIGHT	BUNK
SENSE	CURLEY	GLOVE	FORGOT	FUTURE
WEED	COMPLAIN	BEANS	SMALL	LAND

Of Mice and Men

LENNIE	MILTON	CARLSON	PET	TRAMP
SICK	SALINAS	HEAVEN	GEORGE	BAD
NECK	FRIENDS	FREE SPACE	SOLITAIRE	CAVE
LUGER	SLIM	LAND	SMALL	BEANS
COMPLAIN	WEED	FUTURE	FORGOT	GLOVE

Of Mice and Men

BOSS	CROOKS	NECK	SMALL	PET
TRAMP	JAIL	SALINAS	SLIM	CAVE
CURLEY	GLOVE	FREE SPACE	LAND	MOUSE
HAND	SENSE	BARN	CAMPSITE	BAD
RAPE	CLARA	BEANS	BINDLE	HEAVEN

Of Mice and Men

LENNIE	GEORGE	FUTURE	RABBITS	CANDY
STEINBECK	CARLSON	COMPLAIN	SICK	LUGER
WEED	SOLITAIRE	FREE SPACE	FIGHT	FORGOT
FRIENDS	BUNK	HEAVEN	BINDLE	BEANS
CLARA	RAPE	BAD	CAMPSITE	BARN

Of Mice and Men

RABBITS	SALINAS	CROOKS	RAPE	FORGOT
CLARA	SMALL	LENNIE	CAVE	MOUSE
FUTURE	CURLEY	FREE SPACE	COMPLAIN	PUPPIES
BARN	SOLITAIRE	LAND	HAND	BAD
SICK	WEED	FIGHT	GEORGE	BUNK

Of Mice and Men

CARLSON	BOSS	HEAVEN	SENSE	SLIM
JAIL	PET	LUGER	BINDLE	GLOVE
MILTON	NECK	FREE SPACE	TRAMP	STEINBECK
FRIENDS	CAMPSITE	BUNK	GEORGE	FIGHT
WEED	SICK	BAD	HAND	LAND

Of Mice and Men Vocabulary Word List

No.	Word	Clue/Definition
1.	ANGUISHED	Showing an agonizing physical or mental pain
2.	APPRAISED	Evaluated
3.	APPREHENSIVE	Uneasy; anxious
4.	ASHAMEDLY	Showing a feeling of guilt
5.	BELLIGERENTLY	Hostilely, aggressively
6.	BEMUSED	Put into deep thought
7.	BEWILDERED	Confused; befuddled
8.	COMPLACENTLY	In a self-satisfied manner
9.	CONCEALING	Hiding
10.	CONFIDED	Told private matters not intended to be publicly known
11.	CONSOLED	Comforted
12.	CONTEMPLATED	Considered thoughtfully
13.	CONTEMPTUOUSLY	With a feeling of contempt; scornfully
14.	CONTORTED	Twisted or strained out of shape
15.	DEJECTEDLY	Sadly, depressed or disheartened
16.	DEROGATORY	Detracting or disparaging
17.	DISARMING	Endearing; tending to remove hostility or suspicion
18.	ENTRANCED	Fascinated
19.	GESTURED	Made a motion to express a thought or to emphasize speech
20.	IMPRESSIVELY	Commanding attention; making a strong impression
21.	INDIGNATION	An anger aroused by something unjust, mean or unworthy
22.	MAULED	Handled roughly; beaten up
23.	MEAGER	Deficient in quantity; scant
24.	MIMICKING	Imitating
25.	MOLLIFIED	Pacified; calmed
26.	MONOTONOUS	Unvarying the vocal tone or pitch
27.	MOROSELY	Glumly; gloomily
28.	OMINOUSLY	With foreboding
29.	PANTOMIME	Acting that consists mostly of gesture, no speech
30.	PERSUASIVE	Convincing
31.	PLAINTIVELY	Mournfully; sorrowfully
32.	PRECEDE	Go before
33.	PROFOUND	Complete; coming from the depths of one's being
34.	QUIVERING	Trembling
35.	RELUCTANTLY	Unwillingly; hesitantly
36.	REPREHENSIBLE	Worthy of blame; deserving censure
37.	RETORTED	Sharply replied
38.	SKEPTICALLY	Showing doubt or disbelief; questioningly
39.	SNIVELED	Cried or wept with sniffling
40.	SUBDUED	To quiet or bring under control by physical force
41.	SUBSIDED	Settled down
42.	SULKILY	Gloomily
43.	SULLENNESS	Gloominess
44.	WRITHED	Twisted

Of Mice and Men Vocabulary Fill In The Blanks 1

_____ 1. Complete; coming from the depths of one's being

_____ 2. In a self-satisfied manner

_____ 3. Acting that consists mostly of gesture, no speech

_____ 4. With foreboding

_____ 5. Mournfully; sorrowfully

_____ 6. Imitating

_____ 7. Considered thoughtfully

_____ 8. Hostilely, aggressively

_____ 9. Told private matters not intended to be publicly known

_____ 10. Put into deep thought

_____ 11. Showing doubt or disbelief; questioningly

_____ 12. Commanding attention; making a strong impression

_____ 13. Settled down

_____ 14. Convincing

_____ 15. Showing a feeling of guilt

_____ 16. Showing an agonizing physical or mental pain

_____ 17. Handled roughly; beaten up

_____ 18. Glumly; gloomily

_____ 19. Sadly, depressed or disheartened

_____ 20. Made a motion to express a thought or to emphasize speech

Of Mice and Men Vocabulary Fill In The Blanks 1 Answer Key

PROFOUND	1. Complete; coming from the depths of one's being
COMPLACENTLY	2. In a self-satisfied manner
PANTOMIME	3. Acting that consists mostly of gesture, no speech
OMINOUSLY	4. With foreboding
PLAINTIVELY	5. Mournfully; sorrowfully
MIMICKING	6. Imitating
CONTEMPLATED	7. Considered thoughtfully
BELLIGERENTLY	8. Hostilely, aggressively
CONFIDED	9. Told private matters not intended to be publicly known
BEMUSED	10. Put into deep thought
SKEPTICALLY	11. Showing doubt or disbelief; questioningly
IMPRESSIVELY	12. Commanding attention; making a strong impression
SUBSIDED	13. Settled down
PERSUASIVE	14. Convincing
ASHAMEDLY	15. Showing a feeling of guilt
ANGUISHED	16. Showing an agonizing physical or mental pain
MAULED	17. Handled roughly; beaten up
MOROSELY	18. Glumly; gloomily
DEJECTEDLY	19. Sadly, depressed or disheartened
GESTURED	20. Made a motion to express a thought or to emphasize speech

Of Mice and Men Vocabulary Fill In The Blanks 2

_____ 1. Trembling

_____ 2. Twisted or strained out of shape

_____ 3. Imitating

_____ 4. Endearing; tending to remove hostility or suspicion

_____ 5. Twisted

_____ 6. Fascinated

_____ 7. Worthy of blame; deserving censure

_____ 8. Comforted

_____ 9. Mournfully; sorrowfully

_____ 10. Acting that consists mostly of gesture, no speech

_____ 11. Commanding attention; making a strong impression

_____ 12. Told private matters not intended to be publicly known

_____ 13. Hiding

_____ 14. Gloomily

_____ 15. Unwillingly; hesitantly

_____ 16. To quiet or bring under control by physical force

_____ 17. Sharply replied

_____ 18. Convincing

_____ 19. Showing an agonizing physical or mental pain

_____ 20. An anger aroused by something unjust, mean or unworthy

Of Mice and Men Vocabulary Fill In The Blanks 2 Answer Key

QUIVERING	1. Trembling
CONTORTED	2. Twisted or strained out of shape
MIMICKING	3. Imitating
DISARMING	4. Endearing; tending to remove hostility or suspicion
WRITHED	5. Twisted
ENTRANCED	6. Fascinated
REPREHENSIBLE	7. Worthy of blame; deserving censure
CONSOLED	8. Comforted
PLAINTIVELY	9. Mournfully; sorrowfully
PANTOMIME	10. Acting that consists mostly of gesture, no speech
IMPRESSIVELY	11. Commanding attention; making a strong impression
CONFIDED	12. Told private matters not intended to be publicly known
CONCEALING	13. Hiding
SULKILY	14. Gloomily
RELUCTANTLY	15. Unwillingly; hesitantly
SUBDUED	16. To quiet or bring under control by physical force
RETORTED	17. Sharply replied
PERSUASIVE	18. Convincing
ANGUISHED	19. Showing an agonizing physical or mental pain
INDIGNATION	20. An anger aroused by something unjust, mean or unworthy

Of Mice and Men Vocabulary Fill In The Blanks 3

_____	1. Detracting or disparaging
_____	2. Twisted
_____	3. Go before
_____	4. Sharply replied
_____	5. Mournfully; sorrowfully
_____	6. Twisted or strained out of shape
_____	7. With foreboding
_____	8. Sadly, depressed or disheartened
_____	9. Confused; befuddled
_____	10. Put into deep thought
_____	11. Comforted
_____	12. Told private matters not intended to be publicly known
_____	13. Showing a feeling of guilt
_____	14. Pacified; calmed
_____	15. Endearing; tending to remove hostility or suspicion
_____	16. Settled down
_____	17. With a feeling of contempt; scornfully
_____	18. Unwillingly; hesitantly
_____	19. Fascinated
_____	20. Cried or wept with sniffling

Of Mice and Men Vocabulary Fill In The Blanks 3 Answer Key

DEROGATORY	1. Detracting or disparaging
WRITHED	2. Twisted
PRECEDE	3. Go before
RETORTED	4. Sharply replied
PLAINTIVELY	5. Mournfully; sorrowfully
CONTORTED	6. Twisted or strained out of shape
OMINOUSLY	7. With foreboding
DEJECTEDLY	8. Sadly, depressed or disheartened
BEWILDERED	9. Confused; befuddled
BEMUSED	10. Put into deep thought
CONSOLED	11. Comforted
CONFIDED	12. Told private matters not intended to be publicly known
ASHAMEDLY	13. Showing a feeling of guilt
MOLLIFIED	14. Pacified; calmed
DISARMING	15. Endearing; tending to remove hostility or suspicion
SUBSIDED	16. Settled down
CONTEMPTUOUSLY	17. With a feeling of contempt; scornfully
RELUCTANTLY	18. Unwillingly; hesitantly
ENTRANCED	19. Fascinated
SNIVELED	20. Cried or wept with sniffling

Of Mice and Men Vocabulary Fill In The Blanks 4

_____ 1. Uneasy; anxious

_____ 2. Handled roughly; beaten up

_____ 3. Put into deep thought

_____ 4. Convincing

_____ 5. Gloominess

_____ 6. Twisted or strained out of shape

_____ 7. Worthy of blame; deserving censure

_____ 8. Evaluated

_____ 9. With a feeling of contempt; scornfully

_____ 10. To quiet or bring under control by physical force

_____ 11. Sharply replied

_____ 12. Settled down

_____ 13. Made a motion to express a thought or to emphasize speech

_____ 14. Complete; coming from the depths of one's being

_____ 15. Sadly, depressed or disheartened

_____ 16. An anger aroused by something unjust, mean or unworthy

_____ 17. Mournfully; sorrowfully

_____ 18. Told private matters not intended to be publicly known

_____ 19. Showing doubt or disbelief; questioningly

_____ 20. Showing an agonizing physical or mental pain

Of Mice and Men Vocabulary Fill In The Blanks 4 Answer Key

APPREHENSIVE	1. Uneasy; anxious
MAULED	2. Handled roughly; beaten up
BEMUSED	3. Put into deep thought
PERSUASIVE	4. Convincing
SULLENNESS	5. Gloominess
CONTORTED	6. Twisted or strained out of shape
REPREHENSIBLE	7. Worthy of blame; deserving censure
APPRAISED	8. Evaluated
CONTEMPTUOUSLY	9. With a feeling of contempt; scornfully
SUBDUED	10. To quiet or bring under control by physical force
RETORTED	11. Sharply replied
SUBSIDED	12. Settled down
GESTURED	13. Made a motion to express a thought or to emphasize speech
PROFOUND	14. Complete; coming from the depths of one's being
DEJECTEDLY	15. Sadly, depressed or disheartened
INDIGNATION	16. An anger aroused by something unjust, mean or unworthy
PLAINTIVELY	17. Mournfully; sorrowfully
CONFIDED	18. Told private matters not intended to be publicly known
SKEPTICALLY	19. Showing doubt or disbelief; questioningly
ANGUISHED	20. Showing an agonizing physical or mental pain

Of Mice and Men Vocabulary Matching 1

___ 1. CONTORTED   A. Showing doubt or disbelief; questioningly
___ 2. ASHAMEDLY   B. To quiet or bring under control by physical force
___ 3. SKEPTICALLY   C. Considered thoughtfully
___ 4. PROFOUND   D. Told private matters not intended to be publicly known
___ 5. QUIVERING   E. Imitating
___ 6. PERSUASIVE   F. Hiding
___ 7. ENTRANCED   G. Trembling
___ 8. CONTEMPLATED   H. Gloomily
___ 9. MIMICKING   I. Detracting or disparaging
___10. SUBDUED   J. In a self-satisfied manner
___11. REPREHENSIBLE   K. Hostilely, aggressively
___12. DEROGATORY   L. Showing a feeling of guilt
___13. ANGUISHED   M. Settled down
___14. BELLIGERENTLY   N. Worthy of blame; deserving censure
___15. IMPRESSIVELY   O. Complete; coming from the depths of one's being
___16. COMPLACENTLY   P. Showing an agonizing physical or mental pain
___17. MAULED   Q. Convincing
___18. CONTEMPTUOUSLY   R. Comforted
___19. SULKILY   S. Fascinated
___20. PLAINTIVELY   T. With a feeling of contempt; scornfully
___21. CONCEALING   U. Commanding attention; making a strong impression
___22. INDIGNATION   V. Handled roughly; beaten up
___23. CONFIDED   W. Mournfully; sorrowfully
___24. SUBSIDED   X. Twisted or strained out of shape
___25. CONSOLED   Y. An anger aroused by something unjust, mean or unworthy

Of Mice and Men Vocabulary Matching 1 Answer Key

X - 1. CONTORTED	A.	Showing doubt or disbelief; questioningly
L - 2. ASHAMEDLY	B.	To quiet or bring under control by physical force
A - 3. SKEPTICALLY	C.	Considered thoughtfully
O - 4. PROFOUND	D.	Told private matters not intended to be publicly known
G - 5. QUIVERING	E.	Imitating
Q - 6. PERSUASIVE	F.	Hiding
S - 7. ENTRANCED	G.	Trembling
C - 8. CONTEMPLATED	H.	Gloomily
E - 9. MIMICKING	I.	Detracting or disparaging
B - 10. SUBDUED	J.	In a self-satisfied manner
N - 11. REPREHENSIBLE	K.	Hostilely, aggressively
I - 12. DEROGATORY	L.	Showing a feeling of guilt
P - 13. ANGUISHED	M.	Settled down
K - 14. BELLIGERENTLY	N.	Worthy of blame; deserving censure
U - 15. IMPRESSIVELY	O.	Complete; coming from the depths of one's being
J - 16. COMPLACENTLY	P.	Showing an agonizing physical or mental pain
V - 17. MAULED	Q.	Convincing
T - 18. CONTEMPTUOUSLY	R.	Comforted
H - 19. SULKILY	S.	Fascinated
W - 20. PLAINTIVELY	T.	With a feeling of contempt; scornfully
F - 21. CONCEALING	U.	Commanding attention; making a strong impression
Y - 22. INDIGNATION	V.	Handled roughly; beaten up
D - 23. CONFIDED	W.	Mournfully; sorrowfully
M - 24. SUBSIDED	X.	Twisted or strained out of shape
R - 25. CONSOLED	Y.	An anger aroused by something unjust, mean or unworthy

Of Mice and Men Vocabulary Matching 2

___ 1. QUIVERING   A. Comforted
___ 2. MOROSELY   B. Showing doubt or disbelief; questioningly
___ 3. GESTURED   C. Made a motion to express a thought or to emphasize speech
___ 4. RELUCTANTLY   D. An anger aroused by something unjust, mean or unworthy
___ 5. CONSOLED   E. Evaluated
___ 6. COMPLACENTLY   F. Detracting or disparaging
___ 7. WRITHED   G. Hostilely, aggressively
___ 8. MOLLIFIED   H. Mournfully; sorrowfully
___ 9. PLAINTIVELY   I. With a feeling of contempt; scornfully
___10. CONFIDED   J. Acting that consists mostly of gesture, no speech
___11. SULKILY   K. Confused; befuddled
___12. SULLENNESS   L. Unwillingly; hesitantly
___13. BEWILDERED   M. Gloominess
___14. BELLIGERENTLY   N. Twisted
___15. MAULED   O. Told private matters not intended to be publicly known
___16. CONTEMPTUOUSLY   P. Uneasy; anxious
___17. MIMICKING   Q. Imitating
___18. SKEPTICALLY   R. Handled roughly; beaten up
___19. IMPRESSIVELY   S. Worthy of blame; deserving censure
___20. PANTOMIME   T. Trembling
___21. INDIGNATION   U. Glumly; gloomily
___22. APPRAISED   V. In a self-satisfied manner
___23. REPREHENSIBLE   W. Pacified; calmed
___24. DEROGATORY   X. Commanding attention; making a strong impression
___25. APPREHENSIVE   Y. Gloomily

Of Mice and Men Vocabulary Matching 2 Answer Key

T - 1.	QUIVERING	A. Comforted
U - 2.	MOROSELY	B. Showing doubt or disbelief; questioningly
C - 3.	GESTURED	C. Made a motion to express a thought or to emphasize speech
L - 4.	RELUCTANTLY	D. An anger aroused by something unjust, mean or unworthy
A - 5.	CONSOLED	E. Evaluated
V - 6.	COMPLACENTLY	F. Detracting or disparaging
N - 7.	WRITHED	G. Hostilely, aggressively
W - 8.	MOLLIFIED	H. Mournfully; sorrowfully
H - 9.	PLAINTIVELY	I. With a feeling of contempt; scornfully
O - 10.	CONFIDED	J. Acting that consists mostly of gesture, no speech
Y - 11.	SULKILY	K. Confused; befuddled
M - 12.	SULLENNESS	L. Unwillingly; hesitantly
K - 13.	BEWILDERED	M. Gloominess
G - 14.	BELLIGERENTLY	N. Twisted
R - 15.	MAULED	O. Told private matters not intended to be publicly known
I - 16.	CONTEMPTUOUSLY	P. Uneasy; anxious
Q - 17.	MIMICKING	Q. Imitating
B - 18.	SKEPTICALLY	R. Handled roughly; beaten up
X - 19.	IMPRESSIVELY	S. Worthy of blame; deserving censure
J - 20.	PANTOMIME	T. Trembling
D - 21.	INDIGNATION	U. Glumly; gloomily
E - 22.	APPRAISED	V. In a self-satisfied manner
S - 23.	REPREHENSIBLE	W. Pacified; calmed
F - 24.	DEROGATORY	X. Commanding attention; making a strong impression
P - 25.	APPREHENSIVE	Y. Gloomily

Of Mice and Men Vocabulary Matching 3

____ 1. SNIVELED
____ 2. SUBSIDED
____ 3. SULKILY
____ 4. REPREHENSIBLE
____ 5. OMINOUSLY
____ 6. WRITHED
____ 7. RETORTED
____ 8. APPREHENSIVE
____ 9. MEAGER
____ 10. MAULED
____ 11. BEWILDERED
____ 12. SULLENNESS
____ 13. GESTURED
____ 14. PRECEDE
____ 15. BEMUSED
____ 16. IMPRESSIVELY
____ 17. DEROGATORY
____ 18. MIMICKING
____ 19. CONTORTED
____ 20. SKEPTICALLY
____ 21. CONSOLED
____ 22. BELLIGERENTLY
____ 23. PERSUASIVE
____ 24. APPRAISED
____ 25. PROFOUND

A. Put into deep thought
B. Comforted
C. Convincing
D. Twisted or strained out of shape
E. Detracting or disparaging
F. Twisted
G. Made a motion to express a thought or to emphasize speech
H. With foreboding
I. Cried or wept with sniffling
J. Showing doubt or disbelief; questioningly
K. Complete; coming from the depths of one's being
L. Confused; befuddled
M. Settled down
N. Go before
O. Deficient in quantity; scant
P. Imitating
Q. Hostilely, aggressively
R. Handled roughly; beaten up
S. Sharply replied
T. Gloominess
U. Commanding attention; making a strong impression
V. Gloomily
W. Uneasy; anxious
X. Worthy of blame; deserving censure
Y. Evaluated

Of Mice and Men Vocabulary Matching 3 Answer Key

I - 1. SNIVELED		A. Put into deep thought
M - 2. SUBSIDED		B. Comforted
V - 3. SULKILY		C. Convincing
X - 4. REPREHENSIBLE		D. Twisted or strained out of shape
H - 5. OMINOUSLY		E. Detracting or disparaging
F - 6. WRITHED		F. Twisted
S - 7. RETORTED		G. Made a motion to express a thought or to emphasize speech
W - 8. APPREHENSIVE		H. With foreboding
O - 9. MEAGER		I. Cried or wept with sniffling
R - 10. MAULED		J. Showing doubt or disbelief; questioningly
L - 11. BEWILDERED		K. Complete; coming from the depths of one's being
T - 12. SULLENNESS		L. Confused; befuddled
G - 13. GESTURED		M. Settled down
N - 14. PRECEDE		N. Go before
A - 15. BEMUSED		O. Deficient in quantity; scant
U - 16. IMPRESSIVELY		P. Imitating
E - 17. DEROGATORY		Q. Hostilely, aggressively
P - 18. MIMICKING		R. Handled roughly; beaten up
D - 19. CONTORTED		S. Sharply replied
J - 20. SKEPTICALLY		T. Gloominess
B - 21. CONSOLED		U. Commanding attention; making a strong impression
Q - 22. BELLIGERENTLY		V. Gloomily
C - 23. PERSUASIVE		W. Uneasy; anxious
Y - 24. APPRAISED		X. Worthy of blame; deserving censure
K - 25. PROFOUND		Y. Evaluated

Of Mice and Men Vocabulary Matching 4

___ 1. MONOTONOUS A. Settled down
___ 2. BEMUSED B. Mournfully; sorrowfully
___ 3. BEWILDERED C. Detracting or disparaging
___ 4. PLAINTIVELY D. Go before
___ 5. APPREHENSIVE E. Unwillingly; hesitantly
___ 6. GESTURED F. Told private matters not intended to be publicly known
___ 7. MAULED G. Sharply replied
___ 8. RELUCTANTLY H. Showing a feeling of guilt
___ 9. BELLIGERENTLY I. Fascinated
___10. PRECEDE J. Uneasy; anxious
___11. RETORTED K. Worthy of blame; deserving censure
___12. DEROGATORY L. Confused; befuddled
___13. SUBSIDED M. To quiet or bring under control by physical force
___14. CONSOLED N. Made a motion to express a thought or to emphasize speech
___15. ASHAMEDLY O. Handled roughly; beaten up
___16. COMPLACENTLY P. Twisted
___17. MEAGER Q. Put into deep thought
___18. CONTEMPTUOUSLY R. Imitating
___19. CONFIDED S. Unvarying the vocal tone or pitch
___20. REPREHENSIBLE T. Comforted
___21. SUBDUED U. In a self-satisfied manner
___22. ENTRANCED V. Considered thoughtfully
___23. MIMICKING W. With a feeling of contempt; scornfully
___24. CONTEMPLATED X. Deficient in quantity; scant
___25. WRITHED Y. Hostilely, aggressively

Of Mice and Men Vocabulary Matching 4 Answer Key

S - 1. MONOTONOUS
Q - 2. BEMUSED
L - 3. BEWILDERED
B - 4. PLAINTIVELY
J - 5. APPREHENSIVE
N - 6. GESTURED
O - 7. MAULED
E - 8. RELUCTANTLY
Y - 9. BELLIGERENTLY
D - 10. PRECEDE
G - 11. RETORTED
C - 12. DEROGATORY
A - 13. SUBSIDED
T - 14. CONSOLED
H - 15. ASHAMEDLY
U - 16. COMPLACENTLY
X - 17. MEAGER
W - 18. CONTEMPTUOUSLY
F - 19. CONFIDED
K - 20. REPREHENSIBLE
M - 21. SUBDUED
I - 22. ENTRANCED
R - 23. MIMICKING
V - 24. CONTEMPLATED
P - 25. WRITHED

A. Settled down
B. Mournfully; sorrowfully
C. Detracting or disparaging
D. Go before
E. Unwillingly; hesitantly
F. Told private matters not intended to be publicly known
G. Sharply replied
H. Showing a feeling of guilt
I. Fascinated
J. Uneasy; anxious
K. Worthy of blame; deserving censure
L. Confused; befuddled
M. To quiet or bring under control by physical force
N. Made a motion to express a thought or to emphasize speech
O. Handled roughly; beaten up
P. Twisted
Q. Put into deep thought
R. Imitating
S. Unvarying the vocal tone or pitch
T. Comforted
U. In a self-satisfied manner
V. Considered thoughtfully
W. With a feeling of contempt; scornfully
X. Deficient in quantity; scant
Y. Hostilely, aggressively

Of Mice and Men Vocabulary Magic Squares 1

Match the definition with the vocabulary word. Put your answers in the magic squares below. When your answers are correct, all columns and rows will add to the same number.

A. ASHAMEDLY
B. BEMUSED
C. CONFIDED
D. INDIGNATION
E. WRITHED
F. SUBDUED
G. REPREHENSIBLE
H. APPRAISED
I. MOLLIFIED
J. CONTEMPTUOUSLY
K. GESTURED
L. PERSUASIVE
M. SULLENNESS
N. CONSOLED
O. MOROSELY
P. SNIVELED

1. To quiet or bring under control by physical force
2. Pacified; calmed
3. Glumly; gloomily
4. An anger aroused by something unjust, mean or unworthy
5. Gloominess
6. Put into deep thought
7. Evaluated
8. Made a motion to express a thought or to emphasize speech
9. Told private matters not intended to be publicly known
10. Cried or wept with sniffling
11. With a feeling of contempt; scornfully
12. Twisted
13. Convincing
14. Worthy of blame; deserving censure
15. Showing a feeling of guilt
16. Comforted

A=	B=	C=	D=
E=	F=	G=	H=
I=	J=	K=	L=
M=	N=	O=	P=

Of Mice and Men Vocabulary Magic Squares 1 Answer Key

Match the definition with the vocabulary word. Put your answers in the magic squares below. When your answers are correct, all columns and rows will add to the same number.

A. ASHAMEDLY
B. BEMUSED
C. CONFIDED
D. INDIGNATION
E. WRITHED
F. SUBDUED
G. REPREHENSIBLE
H. APPRAISED
I. MOLLIFIED
J. CONTEMPTUOUSLY
K. GESTURED
L. PERSUASIVE
M. SULLENNESS
N. CONSOLED
O. MOROSELY
P. SNIVELED

1. To quiet or bring under control by physical force
2. Pacified; calmed
3. Glumly; gloomily
4. An anger aroused by something unjust, mean or unworthy
5. Gloominess
6. Put into deep thought
7. Evaluated
8. Made a motion to express a thought or to emphasize speech
9. Told private matters not intended to be publicly known
10. Cried or wept with sniffling
11. With a feeling of contempt; scornfully
12. Twisted
13. Convincing
14. Worthy of blame; deserving censure
15. Showing a feeling of guilt
16. Comforted

A=15	B=6	C=9	D=4
E=12	F=1	G=14	H=7
I=2	J=11	K=8	L=13
M=5	N=16	O=3	P=10

Of Mice and Men Vocabulary Magic Squares 2

Match the definition with the vocabulary word. Put your answers in the magic squares below. When your answers are correct, all columns and rows will add to the same number.

A. MOROSELY
B. PANTOMIME
C. DEROGATORY
D. MOLLIFIED
E. PLAINTIVELY
F. PERSUASIVE
G. MEAGER
H. SKEPTICALLY
I. INDIGNATION
J. CONTEMPLATED
K. WRITHED
L. DISARMING
M. GESTURED
N. BELLIGERENTLY
O. CONCEALING
P. CONFIDED

1. Detracting or disparaging
2. Considered thoughtfully
3. Convincing
4. Hiding
5. Told private matters not intended to be publicly known
6. Mournfully; sorrowfully
7. An anger aroused by something unjust, mean or unworthy
8. Pacified; calmed
9. Made a motion to express a thought or to emphasize speech
10. Showing doubt or disbelief; questioningly
11. Endearing; tending to remove hostility or suspicion
12. Glumly; gloomily
13. Acting that consists mostly of gesture, no speech
14. Twisted
15. Deficient in quantity; scant
16. Hostilely, aggressively

A=	B=	C=	D=
E=	F=	G=	H=
I=	J=	K=	L=
M=	N=	O=	P=

Of Mice and Men Vocabulary Magic Squares 2 Answer Key

Match the definition with the vocabulary word. Put your answers in the magic squares below. When your answers are correct, all columns and rows will add to the same number.

A. MOROSELY
B. PANTOMIME
C. DEROGATORY
D. MOLLIFIED
E. PLAINTIVELY
F. PERSUASIVE
G. MEAGER
H. SKEPTICALLY
I. INDIGNATION
J. CONTEMPLATED
K. WRITHED
L. DISARMING
M. GESTURED
N. BELLIGERENTLY
O. CONCEALING
P. CONFIDED

1. Detracting or disparaging
2. Considered thoughtfully
3. Convincing
4. Hiding
5. Told private matters not intended to be publicly known
6. Mournfully; sorrowfully
7. An anger aroused by something unjust, mean or unworthy
8. Pacified; calmed
9. Made a motion to express a thought or to emphasize speech
10. Showing doubt or disbelief; questioningly
11. Endearing; tending to remove hostility or suspicion
12. Glumly; gloomily
13. Acting that consists mostly of gesture, no speech
14. Twisted
15. Deficient in quantity; scant
16. Hostilely, aggressively

A=12	B=13	C=1	D=8
E=6	F=3	G=15	H=10
I=7	J=2	K=14	L=11
M=9	N=16	O=4	P=5

Of Mice and Men Vocabulary Magic Squares 3

Match the definition with the vocabulary word. Put your answers in the magic squares below. When your answers are correct, all columns and rows will add to the same number.

A. MAULED
B. RETORTED
C. IMPRESSIVELY
D. CONSOLED
E. RELUCTANTLY
F. OMINOUSLY
G. PROFOUND
H. BEMUSED
I. SKEPTICALLY
J. MIMICKING
K. MOROSELY
L. DISARMING
M. SUBDUED
N. BEWILDERED
O. PANTOMIME
P. ENTRANCED

1. To quiet or bring under control by physical force
2. With foreboding
3. Put into deep thought
4. Acting that consists mostly of gesture, no speech
5. Endearing; tending to remove hostility or suspicion
6. Commanding attention; making a strong impression
7. Handled roughly; beaten up
8. Imitating
9. Glumly; gloomily
10. Comforted
11. Sharply replied
12. Showing doubt or disbelief; questioningly
13. Confused; befuddled
14. Unwillingly; hesitantly
15. Complete; coming from the depths of one's being
16. Fascinated

A=	B=	C=	D=
E=	F=	G=	H=
I=	J=	K=	L=
M=	N=	O=	P=

Of Mice and Men Vocabulary Magic Squares 3 Answer Key

Match the definition with the vocabulary word. Put your answers in the magic squares below. When your answers are correct, all columns and rows will add to the same number.

A. MAULED
B. RETORTED
C. IMPRESSIVELY
D. CONSOLED
E. RELUCTANTLY
F. OMINOUSLY
G. PROFOUND
H. BEMUSED
I. SKEPTICALLY
J. MIMICKING
K. MOROSELY
L. DISARMING
M. SUBDUED
N. BEWILDERED
O. PANTOMIME
P. ENTRANCED

1. To quiet or bring under control by physical force
2. With foreboding
3. Put into deep thought
4. Acting that consists mostly of gesture, no speech
5. Endearing; tending to remove hostility or suspicion
6. Commanding attention; making a strong impression
7. Handled roughly; beaten up
8. Imitating
9. Glumly; gloomily
10. Comforted
11. Sharply replied
12. Showing doubt or disbelief; questioningly
13. Confused; befuddled
14. Unwillingly; hesitantly
15. Complete; coming from the depths of one's being
16. Fascinated

A=7	B=11	C=6	D=10
E=14	F=2	G=15	H=3
I=12	J=8	K=9	L=5
M=1	N=13	O=4	P=16

Of Mice and Men Vocabulary Magic Squares 4

Match the definition with the vocabulary word. Put your answers in the magic squares below. When your answers are correct, all columns and rows will add to the same number.

A. BEWILDERED
B. APPRAISED
C. INDIGNATION
D. PROFOUND
E. MEAGER
F. WRITHED
G. DEROGATORY
H. ENTRANCED
I. CONFIDED
J. SULLENNESS
K. CONTEMPLATED
L. ANGUISHED
M. PERSUASIVE
N. RETORTED
O. GESTURED
P. APPREHENSIVE

1. Fascinated
2. Convincing
3. Evaluated
4. Considered thoughtfully
5. Gloominess
6. An anger aroused by something unjust, mean or unworthy
7. Uneasy; anxious
8. Deficient in quantity; scant
9. Made a motion to express a thought or to emphasize speech
10. Twisted
11. Told private matters not intended to be publicly known
12. Complete; coming from the depths of one's being
13. Confused; befuddled
14. Showing an agonizing physical or mental pain
15. Detracting or disparaging
16. Sharply replied

A=	B=	C=	D=
E=	F=	G=	H=
I=	J=	K=	L=
M=	N=	O=	P=

Of Mice and Men Vocabulary Magic Squares 4 Answer Key

Match the definition with the vocabulary word. Put your answers in the magic squares below. When your answers are correct, all columns and rows will add to the same number.

A. BEWILDERED
B. APPRAISED
C. INDIGNATION
D. PROFOUND
E. MEAGER
F. WRITHED
G. DEROGATORY
H. ENTRANCED
I. CONFIDED
J. SULLENNESS
K. CONTEMPLATED
L. ANGUISHED
M. PERSUASIVE
N. RETORTED
O. GESTURED
P. APPREHENSIVE

1. Fascinated
2. Convincing
3. Evaluated
4. Considered thoughtfully
5. Gloominess
6. An anger aroused by something unjust, mean or unworthy
7. Uneasy; anxious
8. Deficient in quantity; scant
9. Made a motion to express a thought or to emphasize speech
10. Twisted
11. Told private matters not intended to be publicly known
12. Complete; coming from the depths of one's being
13. Confused; befuddled
14. Showing an agonizing physical or mental pain
15. Detracting or disparaging
16. Sharply replied

A=13	B=3	C=6	D=12
E=8	F=10	G=15	H=1
I=11	J=5	K=4	L=14
M=2	N=16	O=9	P=7

Of Mice and Men Vocabulary Word Search 1

Words are placed backwards, forward, diagonally, up and down. Clues listed below can help you find the words. Circle the hidden vocabulary words in the maze.

```
C O M P L A C E N T L Y C D E P I G S P
R E L U C T A N T L Y L O E N R N E J J
A N G U I S H E D Y X S N J T O D S H B
S K E P T I C A L L Y U T E R F I T K P
R E T O R T E D W T L O O C A O G U Q T
X F Z M W D G N G N K N R T N U N R P H
N T W Y W P E R B E B I T E C N A E A H
J K W W T Q D R Y R J M E D E D T D N R
T T W Z K H M L O E W O D L D Q I C T Q
S D I S A R M I N G M R K Y K Q O S O P
A U F M M V H Z N I A S I Q H N N U M D
S K B P O Y L I P L U T N T F F B L I D
H U T S R R Z H L L F O I H Z W K M N
A K B B I E O R M E E M D R V E R I E K
M S S D V D C S Y B D E Z P Y E D L G T
E Q J I U M E E D D A P Y F N L Y T C
D S U S F E R D D L J G B E M U S E D J
L Q P B F W D S W E Y E H G V M Q K D Q
Y A P P R A I S E D R R C O N S O L E D
```

Acting that consists mostly of gesture, no speech (9)
An anger aroused by something unjust, mean or unworthy (11)
Comforted (8)
Complete; coming from the depths of one's being (8)
Cried or wept with sniffling (8)
Deficient in quantity; scant (6)
Detracting or disparaging (10)
Endearing; tending to remove hostility or suspicion (9)
Evaluated (9)
Fascinated (9)
Gloomily (7)
Glumly; gloomily (8)
Go before (7)
Handled roughly; beaten up (6)
Hostilely, aggressively (13)
In a self-satisfied manner (12)
Made a motion to express a thought or to emphasize speech (8)

Put into deep thought (7)
Sadly, depressed or disheartened (10)
Settled down (8)
Sharply replied (8)
Showing a feeling of guilt (9)
Showing an agonizing physical or mental pain (9)
Showing doubt or disbelief; questioningly (11)
To quiet or bring under control by physical force (7)
Told private matters not intended to be publicly known (8)
Trembling (9)
Twisted (7)
Twisted or strained out of shape (9)
Unwillingly; hesitantly (11)
With foreboding (9)

Of Mice and Men Vocabulary Word Search 1 Answer Key

Words are placed backwards, forward, diagonally, up and down. Clues listed below can help you find the words. Circle the hidden vocabulary words in the maze.

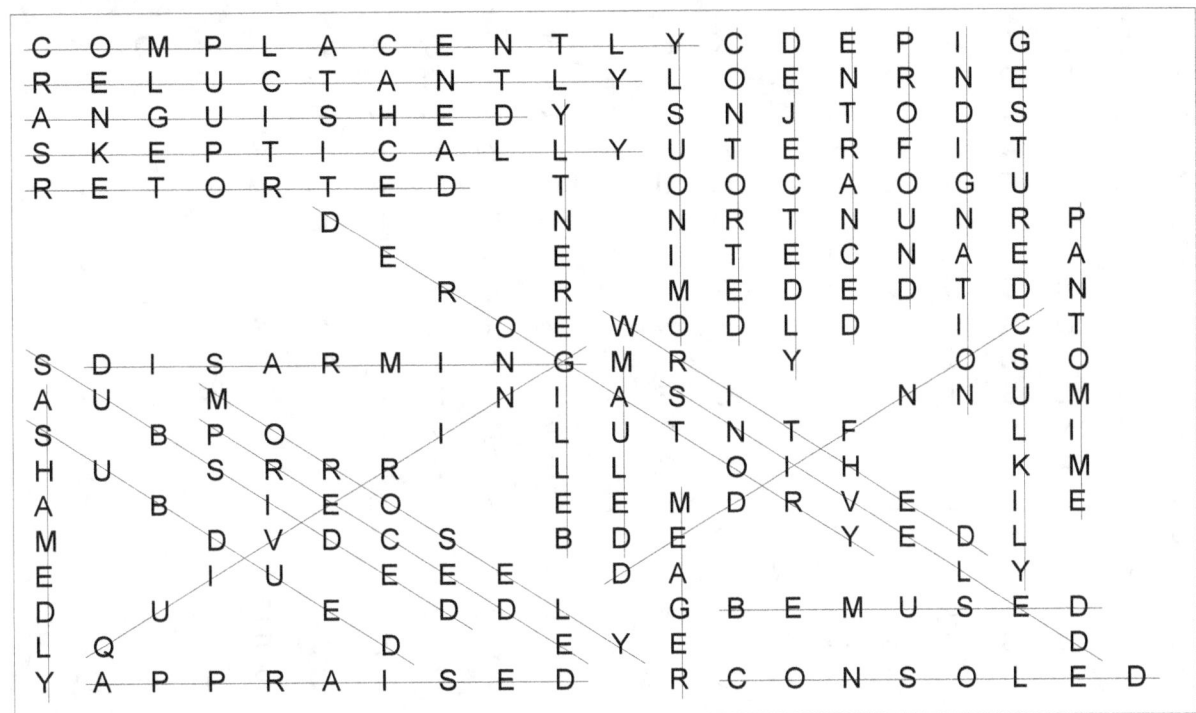

Acting that consists mostly of gesture, no speech (9)
An anger aroused by something unjust, mean or unworthy (11)
Comforted (8)
Complete; coming from the depths of one's being (8)
Cried or wept with sniffling (8)
Deficient in quantity; scant (6)
Detracting or disparaging (10)
Endearing; tending to remove hostility or suspicion (9)
Evaluated (9)
Fascinated (9)
Gloomily (7)
Glumly; gloomily (8)
Go before (7)
Handled roughly; beaten up (6)
Hostilely, aggressively (13)
In a self-satisfied manner (12)
Made a motion to express a thought or to emphasize speech (8)
Put into deep thought (7)
Sadly, depressed or disheartened (10)
Settled down (8)
Sharply replied (8)
Showing a feeling of guilt (9)
Showing an agonizing physical or mental pain (9)
Showing doubt or disbelief; questioningly (11)
To quiet or bring under control by physical force (7)
Told private matters not intended to be publicly known (8)
Trembling (9)
Twisted (7)
Twisted or strained out of shape (9)
Unwillingly; hesitantly (11)
With foreboding (9)

Of Mice and Men Vocabulary Word Search 2

Words are placed backwards, forward, diagonally, up and down. Clues listed below can help you find the words. Circle the hidden vocabulary words in the maze.

```
A M E A G E R S K E P T I C A L L Y O N
W S L P C Z N U P T B V B O P D D C M X
R B H Q R I H B H M E P E M P E S C I M
I L S A V E R D A S M C W P R R V P N R
T R J E M N C U L U U Q I L A O M C O B
H J L V F E L E W L S Q L A I G Z O U Q
E E I I M E D D D L E C D C S A F N S N
D W N S D M Z L G E D J E E E T V T L Z
E C D A U F O L Y N J Y R N D O Y E Y S
R C I U Q B J R B N L C E T M R L M A T
U R G S J X S Q O E J L D L I Y T P N H
T D N R X M B I V S W S M Y M P N T G H
S N A E T R T I D S E J U J I W A U U S
E U T P D C T K W E G L V L C J T O I B
G O I C O N F I D E D G Y W K C C U S J
Y F O X I P A N T O M I M E I I U S H M
T O N A C O N T O R T E D F N T L L E N
W R L S V W Q U I V E R I N G C E Y D S
A P P R E H E N S I V E R E T O R T E D
```

Acting that consists mostly of gesture, no speech (9)
An anger aroused by something unjust, mean or unworthy (11)
Complete; coming from the depths of one's being (8)
Confused; befuddled (10)
Convincing (10)
Cried or wept with sniffling (8)
Deficient in quantity; scant (6)
Detracting or disparaging (10)
Evaluated (9)
Gloomily (7)
Gloominess (10)
Glumly; gloomily (8)
Go before (7)
Handled roughly; beaten up (6)
Imitating (9)
In a self-satisfied manner (12)
Made a motion to express a thought or to emphasize speech (8)
Mournfully; sorrowfully (11)

Put into deep thought (7)
Settled down (8)
Sharply replied (8)
Showing a feeling of guilt (9)
Showing an agonizing physical or mental pain (9)
Showing doubt or disbelief; questioningly (11)
To quiet or bring under control by physical force (7)
Told private matters not intended to be publicly known (8)
Trembling (9)
Twisted (7)
Twisted or strained out of shape (9)
Uneasy; anxious (12)
Unwillingly; hesitantly (11)
With a feeling of contempt; scornfully (14)
With foreboding (9)

Of Mice and Men Vocabulary Word Search 2 Answer Key

Words are placed backwards, forward, diagonally, up and down. Clues listed below can help you find the words. Circle the hidden vocabulary words in the maze.

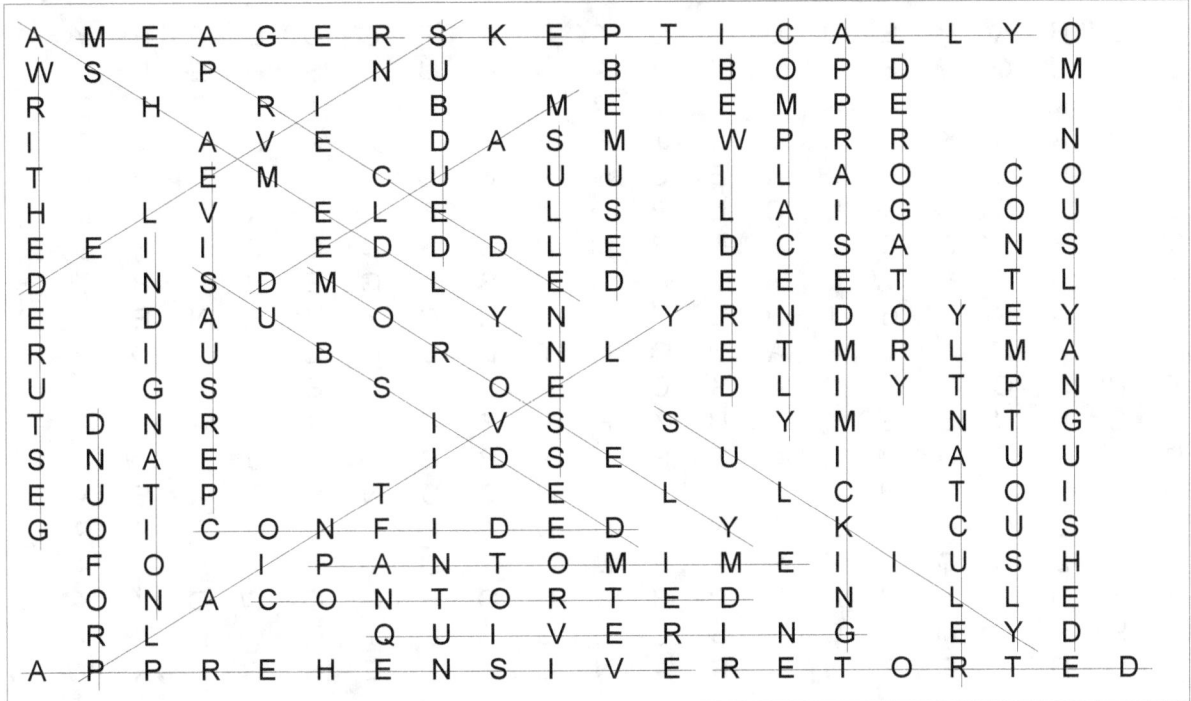

Acting that consists mostly of gesture, no speech (9)
An anger aroused by something unjust, mean or unworthy (11)
Complete; coming from the depths of one's being (8)
Confused; befuddled (10)
Convincing (10)
Cried or wept with sniffling (8)
Deficient in quantity; scant (6)
Detracting or disparaging (10)
Evaluated (9)
Gloomily (7)
Gloominess (10)
Glumly; gloomily (8)
Go before (7)
Handled roughly; beaten up (6)
Imitating (9)
In a self-satisfied manner (12)
Made a motion to express a thought or to emphasize speech (8)
Mournfully; sorrowfully (11)

Put into deep thought (7)
Settled down (8)
Sharply replied (8)
Showing a feeling of guilt (9)
Showing an agonizing physical or mental pain (9)
Showing doubt or disbelief; questioningly (11)
To quiet or bring under control by physical force (7)
Told private matters not intended to be publicly known (8)
Trembling (9)
Twisted (7)
Twisted or strained out of shape (9)
Uneasy; anxious (12)
Unwillingly; hesitantly (11)
With a feeling of contempt; scornfully (14)
With foreboding (9)

Of Mice and Men Vocabulary Word Search 3

Words are placed backwards, forward, diagonally, up and down. Words listed below are included in the maze. Circle the hidden vocabulary words in the maze.

```
A S H A M E D L Y L T N A T C U L E R Y
C N U Q M E X V X P A N G U I S H E D H
O I M L N Q A X T F R P G E S T U R E D
N V A S K R X G S J P E R S U A S I V E
T E U G N I L A E C N O C O N F I D E D
E L L D C M L C L R O O G E F Z X B D M
M E E R S S D Y K F M N B S D O C B E S
P D D Z P W E R Y P O V S X G E U I R T
L E S P X B J N L T G K O Y Y S N E F
A T S M A T E A W Q L T D L L L U D D R
T R E O R N C M X C I F E S S E B I L Y
E O N N L E T X U Z F V T U U S D G I D
D T N O N M E O B S I Y R B O O U N W C
Q E E T S H D H M T E N O S N R E A E X
J R L O K P L B N I D D T I I O D T B R
F Y L N Q W Y I Y F M X N D M M T I X X
B Y U O T N A H D H X E O E O Q W O Y X
S P S U M L B L S C H C C D J R V N T V
Z Q D S P E N T R A N C E D E H T I R W
```

ANGUISHED

ASHAMEDLY

BEMUSED

BEWILDERED

COMPLACENTLY

CONCEALING

CONFIDED

CONSOLED

CONTEMPLATED

CONTORTED

DEJECTEDLY

ENTRANCED

GESTURED

INDIGNATION

MAULED

MEAGER

MOLLIFIED

MONOTONOUS

MOROSELY

OMINOUSLY

PANTOMIME

PERSUASIVE

PLAINTIVELY

PRECEDE

PROFOUND

RELUCTANTLY

RETORTED

SNIVELED

SUBDUED

SUBSIDED

SULKILY

SULLENNESS

WRITHED

Of Mice and Men Vocabulary Word Search 3 Answer Key

Words are placed backwards, forward, diagonally, up and down. Words listed below are included in the maze. Circle the hidden vocabulary words in the maze.

ANGUISHED	ENTRANCED	PLAINTIVELY
ASHAMEDLY	GESTURED	PRECEDE
BEMUSED	INDIGNATION	PROFOUND
BEWILDERED	MAULED	RELUCTANTLY
COMPLACENTLY	MEAGER	RETORTED
CONCEALING	MOLLIFIED	SNIVELED
CONFIDED	MONOTONOUS	SUBDUED
CONSOLED	MOROSELY	SUBSIDED
CONTEMPLATED	OMINOUSLY	SULKILY
CONTORTED	PANTOMIME	SULLENNESS
DEJECTEDLY	PERSUASIVE	WRITHED

Of Mice and Men Vocabulary Word Search 4

Words are placed backwards, forward, diagonally, up and down. Words listed below are included in the maze. Circle the hidden vocabulary words in the maze.

```
D C B E W I L D E R E D E L E V I N S S
E O G Y M S H C J D G N J B V K Q M U P
J N G E S T U R E D D Y S E W G G E L B
E T G M I M I C K I N G U M P V H N L H
C E Q U I V E R I N G A O U N S M T E L
T M G V R R D Y C F S S N S G P S R N R
E P T Z P E T C F H Y Q O E Y W C A N W
D T S S U V B J A X N N T D L R O N E G
L U V D D I D M V G Y B O R E Q N C S R
Y O B F R N E G E R P D N T V D C E S W
S U B S I D E D P A N T O M I M E D D V
S S M Y L I P R M M G R M S T D A E E V
Z L O Y T G J Z C F T E A C N S L L T N
R Y R C O N F I D E D R R U I U I O R V
R J O L J A Z H D N M S O L A L N S O V
R P S H Q T N V L I F F J M L K G N T X
V D E H T I R W N W O B S Q P I L O N N
X M L W K O L G P R Y N J S Z L W C O M
F W Y Y C N A P P R A I S E D Y Y P C M
```

APPRAISED	ENTRANCED	PROFOUND
ASHAMEDLY	GESTURED	QUIVERING
BEMUSED	INDIGNATION	RETORTED
BEWILDERED	MAULED	SNIVELED
CONCEALING	MEAGER	SUBDUED
CONFIDED	MIMICKING	SUBSIDED
CONSOLED	MONOTONOUS	SULKILY
CONTEMPTUOUSLY	MOROSELY	SULLENNESS
CONTORTED	PANTOMIME	WRITHED
DEJECTEDLY	PLAINTIVELY	
DISARMING	PRECEDE	

Of Mice and Men Vocabulary Word Search 4 Answer Key

Words are placed backwards, forward, diagonally, up and down. Words listed below are included in the maze. Circle the hidden vocabulary words in the maze.

APPRAISED	ENTRANCED	PROFOUND
ASHAMEDLY	GESTURED	QUIVERING
BEMUSED	INDIGNATION	RETORTED
BEWILDERED	MAULED	SNIVELED
CONCEALING	MEAGER	SUBDUED
CONFIDED	MIMICKING	SUBSIDED
CONSOLED	MONOTONOUS	SULKILY
CONTEMPTUOUSLY	MOROSELY	SULLENNESS
CONTORTED	PANTOMIME	WRITHED
DEJECTEDLY	PLAINTIVELY	
DISARMING	PRECEDE	

Of Mice and Men Vocabulary Crossword 1

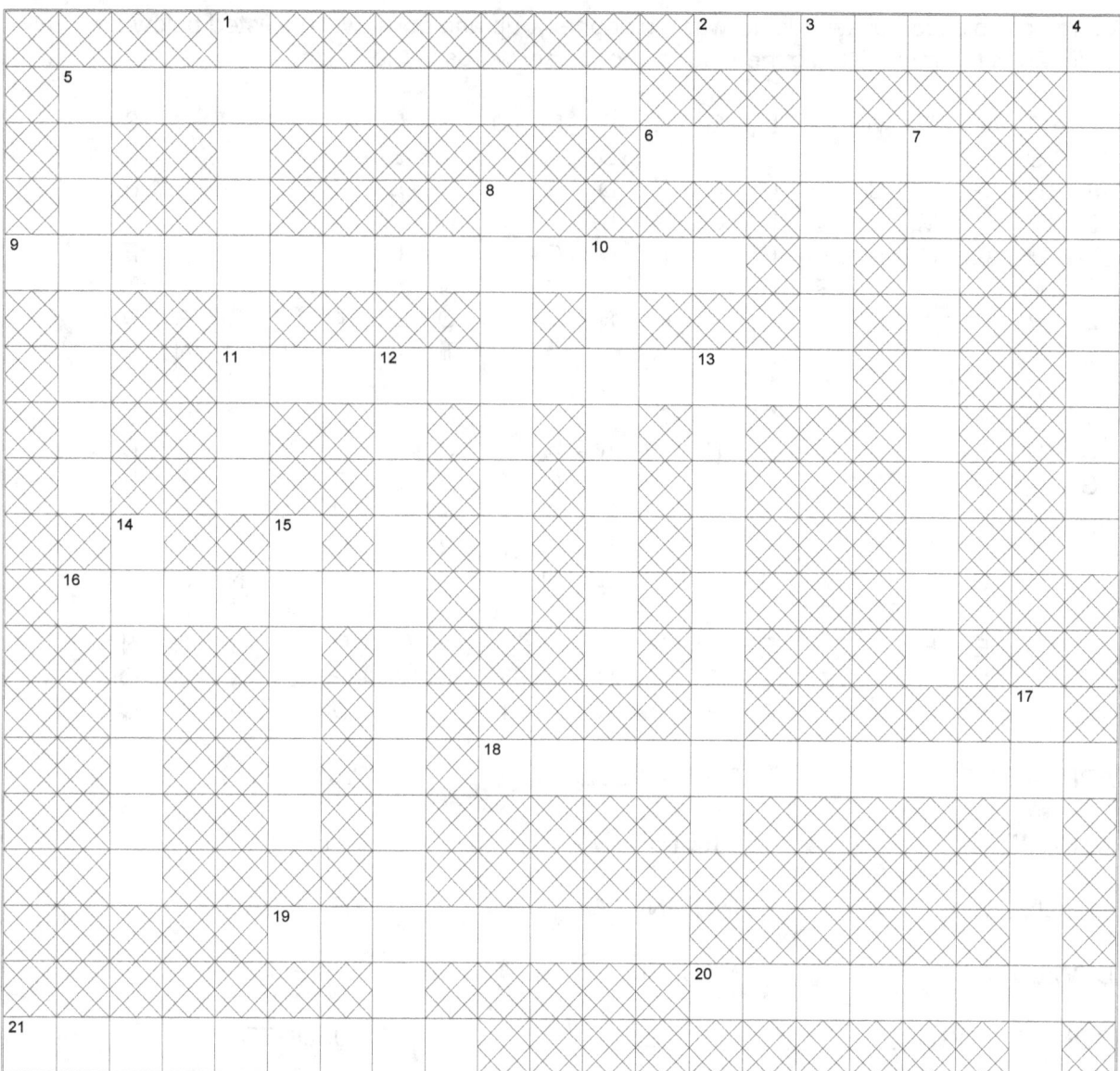

Across
2. Made a motion to express a thought or to emphasize speech
5. Unwillingly; hesitantly
6. Handled roughly; beaten up
9. With a feeling of contempt; scornfully
11. Commanding attention; making a strong impression
16. Go before
18. Considered thoughtfully
19. Settled down
20. Told private matters not intended to be publicly known
21. Pacified; calmed

Down
1. Trembling
3. Gloomily
4. Detracting or disparaging
5. Sharply replied
7. Sadly, depressed or disheartened
8. Comforted
10. Cried or wept with sniffling
12. Worthy of blame; deserving censure
13. Fascinated
14. Twisted
15. Deficient in quantity; scant
17. Put into deep thought

Of Mice and Men Vocabulary Crossword 1 Answer Key

			¹Q					²G	³S	T	U	R	E	⁴D
	⁵R	E	L	U	C	T	A	N	T	L	Y		U			E
	E		I					⁶M	A	U	L	E	⁷D		R
	T		V				⁸C			K		E		O
⁹C	O	N	T	E	M	P	T	U	O	¹⁰S	L	Y		I		J		G
	R		R				N		N		L		E		A
	T		¹¹I	M	¹²P	R	E	S	S	¹³I	V	E	L	Y		C		T
	E		N		R		E		O		V		N		T		O
	D		G		E		P		L		E		T		E		R
		¹⁴W		¹⁵M		R		E		L		R		D		Y
	¹⁶P	R	E	C	E	D	E		D		E		A		L
		I		A		H				D		N		Y
		T		G		E						C			¹⁷B
		H		E		N		¹⁸C	O	N	T	E	M	P	L	A	T	E	D
		E		R		S						D		M
		D				I								U
			¹⁹S	U	B	S	I	D	E	D				S
						L				²⁰C	O	N	F	I	D	E	D
²¹M	O	L	L	I	F	I	E	D						D

Across
2. Made a motion to express a thought or to emphasize speech
5. Unwillingly; hesitantly
6. Handled roughly; beaten up
9. With a feeling of contempt; scornfully
11. Commanding attention; making a strong impression
16. Go before
18. Considered thoughtfully
19. Settled down
20. Told private matters not intended to be publicly known
21. Pacified; calmed

Down
1. Trembling
3. Gloomily
4. Detracting or disparaging
5. Sharply replied
7. Sadly, depressed or disheartened
8. Comforted
10. Cried or wept with sniffling
12. Worthy of blame; deserving censure
13. Fascinated
14. Twisted
15. Deficient in quantity; scant
17. Put into deep thought

Of Mice and Men Vocabulary Crossword 2

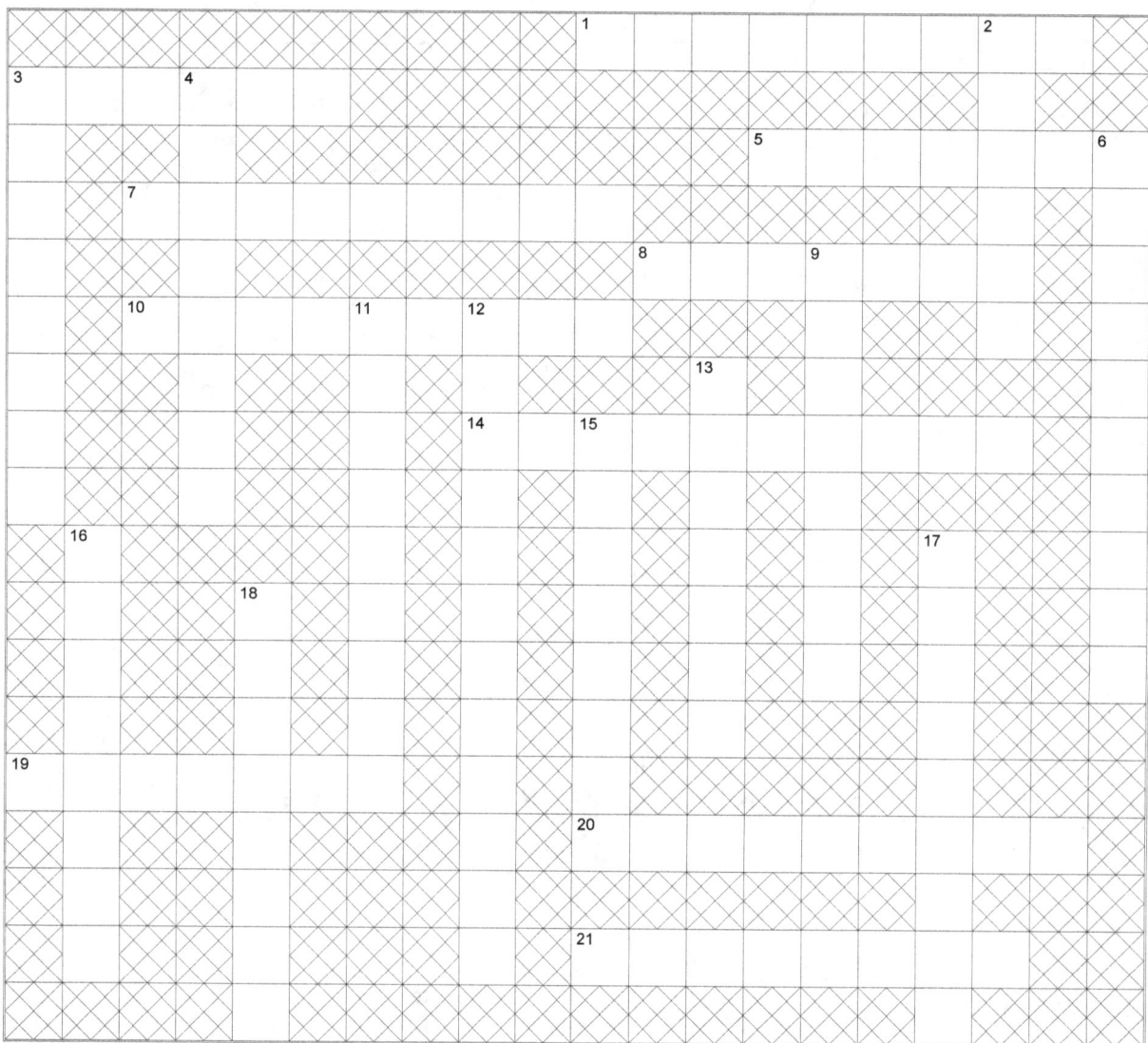

Across
1. Acting that consists mostly of gesture, no speech
3. Deficient in quantity; scant
5. To quiet or bring under control by physical force
7. Showing a feeling of guilt
8. Go before
10. Trembling
14. Convincing
19. Put into deep thought
20. Endearing; tending to remove hostility or suspicion
21. Told private matters not intended to be publicly known

Down
2. Handled roughly; beaten up
3. Glumly; gloomily
4. Made a motion to express a thought or to emphasize speech
6. Detracting or disparaging
9. Comforted
11. Fascinated
12. Commanding attention; making a strong impression
13. Gloomily
15. Sharply replied
16. Cried or wept with sniffling
17. Evaluated
18. Settled down

Of Mice and Men Vocabulary Crossword 2 Answer Key

Across
1. Acting that consists mostly of gesture, no speech
3. Deficient in quantity; scant
5. To quiet or bring under control by physical force
7. Showing a feeling of guilt
8. Go before
10. Trembling
14. Convincing
19. Put into deep thought
20. Endearing; tending to remove hostility or suspicion
21. Told private matters not intended to be publicly known

Down
2. Handled roughly; beaten up
3. Glumly; gloomily
4. Made a motion to express a thought or to emphasize speech
6. Detracting or disparaging
9. Comforted
11. Fascinated
12. Commanding attention; making a strong impression
13. Gloomily
15. Sharply replied
16. Cried or wept with sniffling
17. Evaluated
18. Settled down

Of Mice and Men Vocabulary Crossword 3

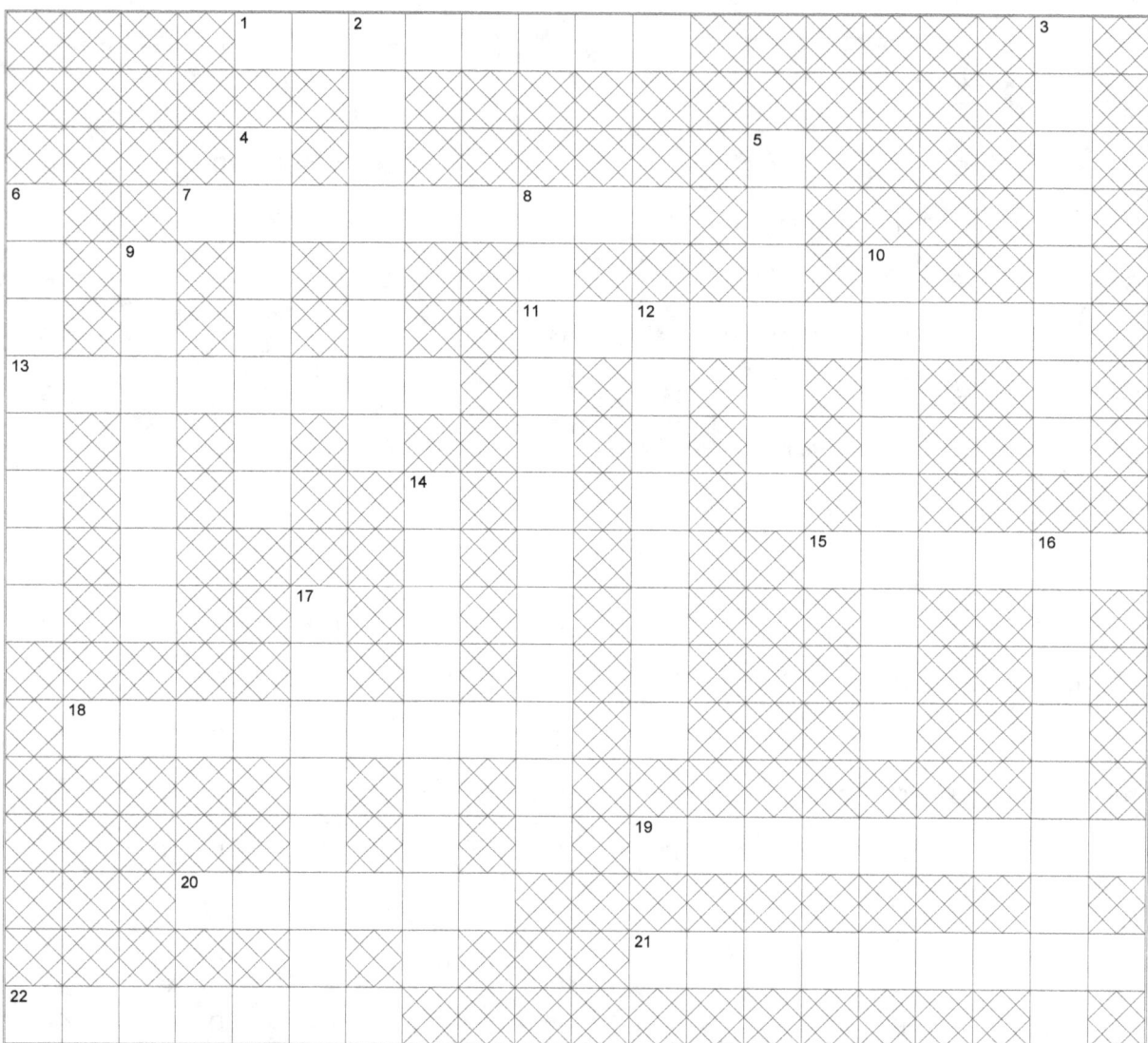

Across
1. Made a motion to express a thought or to emphasize speech
7. Trembling
11. Convincing
13. Settled down
15. Deficient in quantity; scant
18. Acting that consists mostly of gesture, no speech
19. Endearing; tending to remove hostility or suspicion
20. Handled roughly; beaten up
21. Evaluated
22. Go before

Down
2. Cried or wept with sniffling
3. Glumly; gloomily
4. Gloomily
5. Put into deep thought
6. Comforted
8. Commanding attention; making a strong impression
9. To quiet or bring under control by physical force
10. Showing a feeling of guilt
12. Sharply replied
14. Pacified; calmed
16. Fascinated
17. Complete; coming from the depths of one's being

Of Mice and Men Vocabulary Crossword 3 Answer Key

```
            1G E 2S T U R E D           3M
                  N                      O
         4S       I              5B      R
6C    7Q U I V E R  8I  N  G     E       O
 O  9S    L     E    M           M  10A  S
 N   U    K     L   11P E 12R S U A S I V E
13S U B S I D E D    R       E      H     L
 O   D    L     D    E       T      A     Y
 L   U    Y    14M   S       O      D
 E   E          O    S       R   15M E A 16G E R
 D   D        17P    L       I      D         N
              R      L       E      L         T
     18P A N T O M I M E     D      Y         R
              F      F                        A
              O      I      19D I S A R M I N G
           20M A U L E D                      C
              N      D      21A P P R A I S E D
22P R E C E D E                               D
```

Across
1. Made a motion to express a thought or to emphasize speech
7. Trembling
11. Convincing
13. Settled down
15. Deficient in quantity; scant
18. Acting that consists mostly of gesture, no speech
19. Endearing; tending to remove hostility or suspicion
20. Handled roughly; beaten up
21. Evaluated
22. Go before

Down
2. Cried or wept with sniffling
3. Glumly; gloomily
4. Gloomily
5. Put into deep thought
6. Comforted
8. Commanding attention; making a strong impression
9. To quiet or bring under control by physical force
10. Showing a feeling of guilt
12. Sharply replied
14. Pacified; calmed
16. Fascinated
17. Complete; coming from the depths of one's being

Of Mice and Men Vocabulary Crossword 4

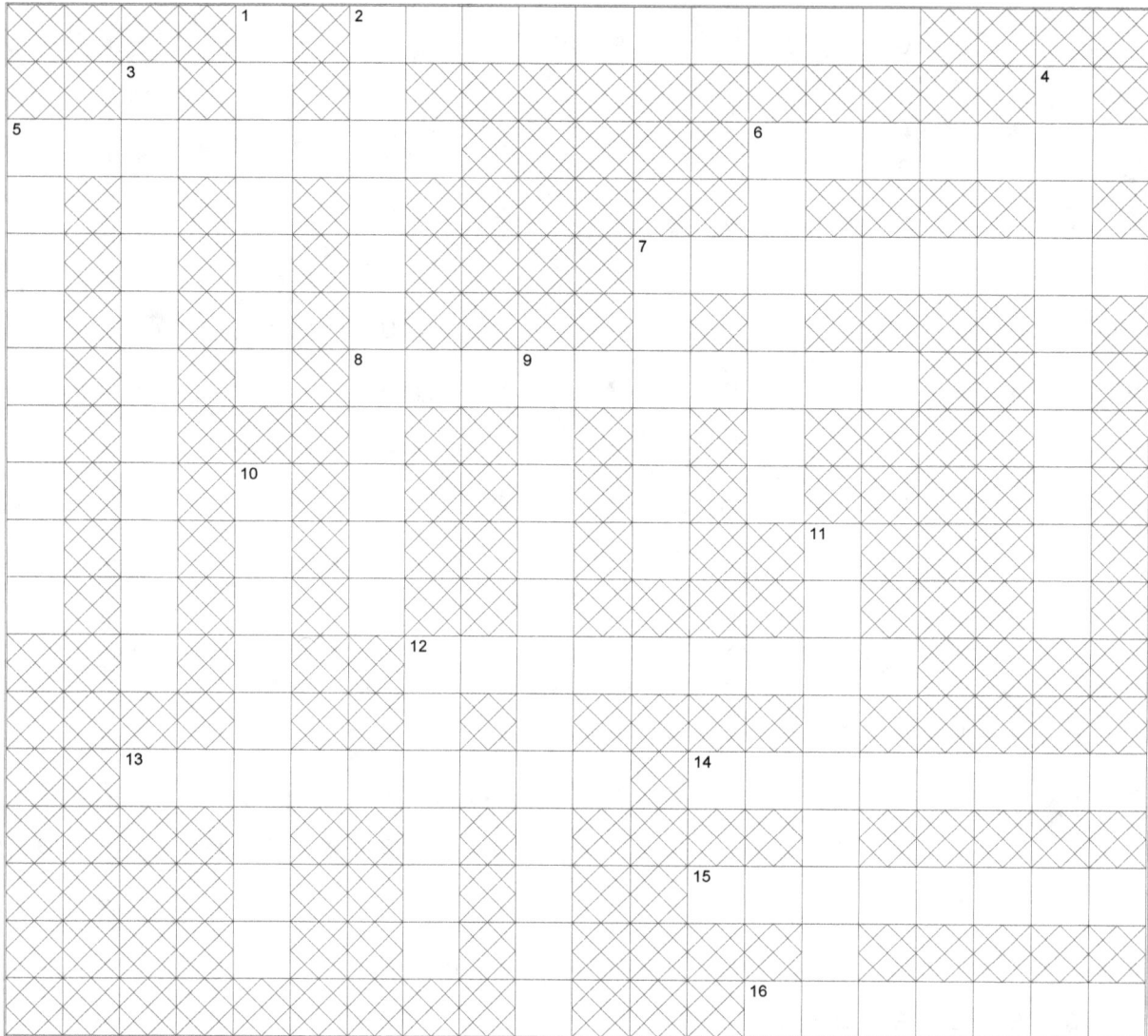

Across
2. Gloominess
5. Told private matters not intended to be publicly known
6. To quiet or bring under control by physical force
7. Pacified; calmed
8. Hiding
12. Imitating
13. With foreboding
14. Complete; coming from the depths of one's being
15. Cried or wept with sniffling
16. Put into deep thought

Down
1. Twisted
2. Showing doubt or disbelief; questioningly
3. An anger aroused by something unjust, mean or unworthy
4. Sadly, depressed or disheartened
5. Twisted or strained out of shape
6. Gloomily
7. Deficient in quantity; scant
9. Considered thoughtfully
10. Evaluated
11. Acting that consists mostly of gesture, no speech
12. Handled roughly; beaten up

Of Mice and Men Vocabulary Crossword 4 Answer Key

Across
2. Gloominess
5. Told private matters not intended to be publicly known
6. To quiet or bring under control by physical force
7. Pacified; calmed
8. Hiding
12. Imitating
13. With foreboding
14. Complete; coming from the depths of one's being
15. Cried or wept with sniffling
16. Put into deep thought

Down
1. Twisted
2. Showing doubt or disbelief; questioningly
3. An anger aroused by something unjust, mean or unworthy
4. Sadly, depressed or disheartened
5. Twisted or strained out of shape
6. Gloomily
7. Deficient in quantity; scant
9. Considered thoughtfully
10. Evaluated
11. Acting that consists mostly of gesture, no speech
12. Handled roughly; beaten up

Of Mice and Men Vocabulary Juggle Letters 1

1. EBDWEEIDLR = 1. _____
   Confused; befuddled

2. AENRETNDC = 2. _____
   Fascinated

3. AEOCCNGNLI = 3. _____
   Hiding

4. PEPASAIDR = 4. _____
   Evaluated

5. EBSDMUE = 5. _____
   Put into deep thought

6. EORNOCDTT = 6. _____
   Twisted or strained out of shape

7. EDLUMA = 7. _____
   Handled roughly; beaten up

8. IMIGICMKN = 8. _____
   Imitating

9. IEWRHDT = 9. _____
   Twisted

10. EMSILERPSIVY = 10. _____
    Commanding attention; making a strong impression

11. LELUSENSNS = 11. _____
    Gloominess

12. NIGYBLLELETRE = 12. _____
    Hostilely, aggressively

13. REGMAE = 13. _____
    Deficient in quantity; scant

14. NIEVAPTYLIL = 14. _____
    Mournfully; sorrowfully

15. LPTEDMNCOTEA = 15. _____
    Considered thoughtfully

Of Mice and Men Vocabulary Juggle Letters 1 Answer Key

1. EBDWEEIDLR = 1. BEWILDERED
Confused; befuddled

2. AENRETNDC = 2. ENTRANCED
Fascinated

3. AEOCCNGNLI = 3. CONCEALING
Hiding

4. PEPASAIDR = 4. APPRAISED
Evaluated

5. EBSDMUE = 5. BEMUSED
Put into deep thought

6. EORNOCDTT = 6. CONTORTED
Twisted or strained out of shape

7. EDLUMA = 7. MAULED
Handled roughly; beaten up

8. IMIGICMKN = 8. MIMICKING
Imitating

9. IEWRHDT = 9. WRITHED
Twisted

10. EMSILERPSIVY =10. IMPRESSIVELY
Commanding attention; making a strong impression

11. LELUSENSNS =11. SULLENNESS
Gloominess

12. NIGYBLLELETRE =12. BELLIGERENTLY
Hostilely, aggressively

13. REGMAE =13. MEAGER
Deficient in quantity; scant

14. NIEVAPTYLIL =14. PLAINTIVELY
Mournfully; sorrowfully

15. LPTEDMNCOTEA =15. CONTEMPLATED
Considered thoughtfully

Of Mice and Men Vocabulary Juggle Letters 2

1. LYSUILK = 1. _____
   Gloomily

2. RDOERETT = 2. _____
   Sharply replied

3. EPMMOIATN = 3. _____
   Acting that consists mostly of gesture, no speech

4. ETYRADOOGR = 4. _____
   Detracting or disparaging

5. DSDSEUBI = 5. _____
   Settled down

6. OTRENTCDO = 6. _____
   Twisted or strained out of shape

7. LTCSEKPYALI = 7. _____
   Showing doubt or disbelief; questioningly

8. ILDIFLMOE = 8. _____
   Pacified; calmed

9. HALSMYEDA = 9. _____
   Showing a feeling of guilt

10. HLEIPEBSRENRE =10. _____
    Worthy of blame; deserving censure

11. LNENICACOG =11. _____
    Hiding

12. IMIGDRSAN =12. _____
    Endearing; tending to remove hostility or suspicion

13. DEVNIELS =13. _____
    Cried or wept with sniffling

14. ELEDREDWBI =14. _____
    Confused; befuddled

15. IGDNOIINNTA =15. _____
    An anger aroused by something unjust, mean or unworthy

Of Mice and Men Vocabulary Juggle Letters 2 Answer Key

1. LYSUILK = 1. SULKILY
   Gloomily

2. RDOERETT = 2. RETORTED
   Sharply replied

3. EPMMOIATN = 3. PANTOMIME
   Acting that consists mostly of gesture, no speech

4. ETYRADOOGR = 4. DEROGATORY
   Detracting or disparaging

5. DSDSEUBI = 5. SUBSIDED
   Settled down

6. OTRENTCDO = 6. CONTORTED
   Twisted or strained out of shape

7. LTCSEKPYALI = 7. SKEPTICALLY
   Showing doubt or disbelief; questioningly

8. ILDIFLMOE = 8. MOLLIFIED
   Pacified; calmed

9. HALSMYEDA = 9. ASHAMEDLY
   Showing a feeling of guilt

10. HLEIPEBSRENRE =10. REPREHENSIBLE
    Worthy of blame; deserving censure

11. LNENICACOG =11. CONCEALING
    Hiding

12. IMIGDRSAN =12. DISARMING
    Endearing; tending to remove hostility or suspicion

13. DEVNIELS =13. SNIVELED
    Cried or wept with sniffling

14. ELEDREDWBI =14. BEWILDERED
    Confused; befuddled

15. IGDNOIINNTA =15. INDIGNATION
    An anger aroused by something unjust, mean or unworthy

Of Mice and Men Vocabulary Juggle Letters 3

1. IKNIMGMCI = 1. _____
   Imitating

2. CREEPED = 2. _____
   Go before

3. IPIMESLVESYR = 3. _____
   Commanding attention; making a strong impression

4. OTEETRDR = 4. _____
   Sharply replied

5. UMOONUYPLSETTC = 5. _____
   With a feeling of contempt; scornfully

6. ROLSEOYM = 6. _____
   Glumly; gloomily

7. OTNOSMOUNO = 7. _____
   Unvarying the vocal tone or pitch

8. UEBMESD = 8. _____
   Put into deep thought

9. TENYCPLALMCO = 9. _____
   In a self-satisfied manner

10. HISDNGUEA =10. _____
    Showing an agonizing physical or mental pain

11. LETJDEDCYE =11. _____
    Sadly, depressed or disheartened

12. DWHIERT =12. _____
    Twisted

13. NIEGVRQUI =13. _____
    Trembling

14. HEADSALMY =14. _____
    Showing a feeling of guilt

15. YAODEROTGR =15. _____
    Detracting or disparaging

Of Mice and Men Vocabulary Juggle Letters 3 Answer Key

1. IKNIMGMCI = 1. MIMICKING
Imitating

2. CREEPED = 2. PRECEDE
Go before

3. IPIMESLVESYR = 3. IMPRESSIVELY
Commanding attention; making a strong impression

4. OTEETRDR = 4. RETORTED
Sharply replied

5. UMOONUYPLSETTC = 5. CONTEMPTUOUSLY
With a feeling of contempt; scornfully

6. ROLSEOYM = 6. MOROSELY
Glumly; gloomily

7. OTNOSMOUNO = 7. MONOTONOUS
Unvarying the vocal tone or pitch

8. UEBMESD = 8. BEMUSED
Put into deep thought

9. TENYCPLALMCO = 9. COMPLACENTLY
In a self-satisfied manner

10. HISDNGUEA =10. ANGUISHED
Showing an agonizing physical or mental pain

11. LETJDEDCYE =11. DEJECTEDLY
Sadly, depressed or disheartened

12. DWHIERT =12. WRITHED
Twisted

13. NIEGVRQUI =13. QUIVERING
Trembling

14. HEADSALMY =14. ASHAMEDLY
Showing a feeling of guilt

15. YAODEROTGR =15. DEROGATORY
Detracting or disparaging

Of Mice and Men Vocabulary Juggle Letters 4

1. MSYULIONO = 1. _____
   With foreboding

2. EURDTEGS = 2. _____
   Made a motion to express a thought or to emphasize speech

3. DLJECTDYEE = 3. _____
   Sadly, depressed or disheartened

4. UTUEMCYONLOSPT = 4. _____
   With a feeling of contempt; scornfully

5. FIDIOLEML = 5. _____
   Pacified, calmed

6. RDAIPSPEA = 6. _____
   Evaluated

7. EDAMYSLAH = 7. _____
   Showing a feeling of guilt

8. OOCSEDLN = 8. _____
   Comforted

9. NPLIITEYAVL = 9. _____
   Mournfully; sorrowfully

10. SVEAUIPERS = 10. _____
    Convincing

11. AGMREE = 11. _____
    Deficient in quantity; scant

12. OEMPNMATI = 12. _____
    Acting that consists mostly of gesture, no speech

13. RESPSIMYVEIL = 13. _____
    Commanding attention; making a strong impression

14. GVEIQIRUN = 14. _____
    Trembling

15. USSDDIBE = 15. _____
    Settled down

Of Mice and Men Vocabulary Juggle Letters 4 Answer Key

1. MSYULIONO = 1. OMINOUSLY
   With foreboding

2. EURDTEGS = 2. GESTURED
   Made a motion to express a thought or to emphasize speech

3. DLJECTDYEE = 3. DEJECTEDLY
   Sadly, depressed or disheartened

4. UTUEMCYONLOSPT = 4. CONTEMPTUOUSLY
   With a feeling of contempt; scornfully

5. FIDIOLEML = 5. MOLLIFIED
   Pacified, calmed

6. RDAIPSPEA = 6. APPRAISED
   Evaluated

7. EDAMYSLAH = 7. ASHAMEDLY
   Showing a feeling of guilt

8. OOCSEDLN = 8. CONSOLED
   Comforted

9. NPLIITEYAVL = 9. PLAINTIVELY
   Mournfully; sorrowfully

10. SVEAUIPERS =10. PERSUASIVE
    Convincing

11. AGMREE =11. MEAGER
    Deficient in quantity; scant

12. OEMPNMATI =12. PANTOMIME
    Acting that consists mostly of gesture, no speech

13. RESPSIMYVEIL =13. IMPRESSIVELY
    Commanding attention; making a strong impression

14. GVEIQIRUN =14. QUIVERING
    Trembling

15. USSDDIBE =15. SUBSIDED
    Settled down

ANGUISHED	Showing an agonizing physical or mental pain
APPRAISED	Evaluated
APPREHENSIVE	Uneasy; anxious
ASHAMEDLY	Showing a feeling of guilt
BELLIGERENTLY	Hostilely, aggressively
BEMUSED	Put into deep thought

BEWILDERED	Confused; befuddled
COMPLACENTLY	In a self-satisfied manner
CONCEALING	Hiding
CONFIDED	Told private matters not intended to be publicly known
CONSOLED	Comforted
CONTEMPLATED	Considered thoughtfully

CONTEMPTUOUSLY	With a feeling of contempt; scornfully
CONTORTED	Twisted or strained out of shape
DEJECTEDLY	Sadly, depressed or disheartened
DEROGATORY	Detracting or disparaging
DISARMING	Endearing; tending to remove hostility or suspicion
ENTRANCED	Fascinated

GESTURED	Made a motion to express a thought or to emphasize speech
IMPRESSIVELY	Commanding attention; making a strong impression
INDIGNATION	An anger aroused by something unjust, mean or unworthy
MAULED	Handled roughly; beaten up
MEAGER	Deficient in quantity; scant
MIMICKING	Imitating

MOLLIFIED	Pacified; calmed
MONOTONOUS	Unvarying the vocal tone or pitch
MOROSELY	Glumly; gloomily
OMINOUSLY	With foreboding
PANTOMIME	Acting that consists mostly of gesture, no speech
PERSUASIVE	Convincing

PLAINTIVELY	Mournfully; sorrowfully
PRECEDE	Go before
PROFOUND	Complete; coming from the depths of one's being
QUIVERING	Trembling
RELUCTANTLY	Unwillingly; hesitantly
REPREHENSIBLE	Worthy of blame; deserving censure

RETORTED	Sharply replied
SKEPTICALLY	Showing doubt or disbelief; questioningly
SNIVELED	Cried or wept with sniffling
SUBDUED	To quiet or bring under control by physical force
SUBSIDED	Settled down
SULKILY	Gloomily

SULLENNESS	Gloominess
WRITHED	Twisted

Of Mice and Men Vocabulary

PROFOUND	BELLIGERENTLY	SULKILY	MONOTONOUS	SNIVELED
BEWILDERED	SUBSIDED	MAULED	DEROGATORY	CONTORTED
CONTEMPTUOUSLY	OMINOUSLY	FREE SPACE	SKEPTICALLY	PRECEDE
COMPLACENTLY	RETORTED	PANTOMIME	QUIVERING	APPRAISED
MEAGER	DISARMING	DEJECTEDLY	MOROSELY	SUBDUED

Of Mice and Men Vocabulary

CONTEMPLATED	ENTRANCED	WRITHED	CONFIDED	REPREHENSIBLE
SULLENNESS	INDIGNATION	MOLLIFIED	CONCEALING	PLAINTIVELY
RELUCTANTLY	ASHAMEDLY	FREE SPACE	APPREHENSIVE	GESTURED
BEMUSED	CONSOLED	PERSUASIVE	MIMICKING	SUBDUED
MOROSELY	DEJECTEDLY	DISARMING	MEAGER	APPRAISED

Of Mice and Men Vocabulary

GESTURED	REPREHENSIBLE	ASHAMEDLY	CONSOLED	SULKILY
MOROSELY	APPREHENSIVE	SULLENNESS	MEAGER	RETORTED
ENTRANCED	CONCEALING	FREE SPACE	RELUCTANTLY	SUBDUED
DEROGATORY	PROFOUND	MIMICKING	OMINOUSLY	MAULED
DISARMING	CONTEMPLATED	IMPRESSIVELY	APPRAISED	WRITHED

Of Mice and Men Vocabulary

INDIGNATION	PLAINTIVELY	PERSUASIVE	QUIVERING	PRECEDE
CONFIDED	DEJECTEDLY	MONOTONOUS	SNIVELED	CONTEMPTUOUSLY
MOLLIFIED	COMPLACENTLY	FREE SPACE	BELLIGERENTLY	PANTOMIME
BEWILDERED	SKEPTICALLY	BEMUSED	ANGUISHED	WRITHED
APPRAISED	IMPRESSIVELY	CONTEMPLATED	DISARMING	MAULED

Of Mice and Men Vocabulary

PLAINTIVELY	INDIGNATION	DEROGATORY	SNIVELED	SUBSIDED
SUBDUED	RETORTED	PERSUASIVE	APPRAISED	IMPRESSIVELY
BEWILDERED	QUIVERING	FREE SPACE	COMPLACENTLY	CONTEMPTUOUSLY
PANTOMIME	CONTEMPLATED	DEJECTEDLY	OMINOUSLY	ENTRANCED
CONTORTED	CONCEALING	BELLIGERENTLY	PROFOUND	MOROSELY

Of Mice and Men Vocabulary

CONFIDED	MAULED	MONOTONOUS	CONSOLED	MOLLIFIED
APPREHENSIVE	RELUCTANTLY	SULKILY	BEMUSED	ASHAMEDLY
ANGUISHED	WRITHED	FREE SPACE	SKEPTICALLY	REPREHENSIBLE
MIMICKING	SULLENNESS	DISARMING	MEAGER	MOROSELY
PROFOUND	BELLIGERENTLY	CONCEALING	CONTORTED	ENTRANCED

Of Mice and Men Vocabulary

CONTEMPLATED	BEWILDERED	DEROGATORY	CONCEALING	SUBSIDED
DEJECTEDLY	SKEPTICALLY	BELLIGERENTLY	REPREHENSIBLE	BEMUSED
SULKILY	PANTOMIME	FREE SPACE	PRECEDE	RETORTED
MONOTONOUS	SULLENNESS	MIMICKING	MEAGER	CONFIDED
SNIVELED	GESTURED	ANGUISHED	IMPRESSIVELY	CONTEMPTUOUSLY

Of Mice and Men Vocabulary

RELUCTANTLY	MAULED	QUIVERING	DISARMING	APPREHENSIVE
MOLLIFIED	MOROSELY	PLAINTIVELY	WRITHED	OMINOUSLY
APPRAISED	CONTORTED	FREE SPACE	COMPLACENTLY	ENTRANCED
CONSOLED	PROFOUND	SUBDUED	PERSUASIVE	CONTEMPTUOUSLY
IMPRESSIVELY	ANGUISHED	GESTURED	SNIVELED	CONFIDED

Of Mice and Men Vocabulary

PLAINTIVELY	SULLENNESS	CONFIDED	MAULED	RETORTED
PRECEDE	WRITHED	OMINOUSLY	REPREHENSIBLE	BEWILDERED
BEMUSED	SULKILY	FREE SPACE	CONCEALING	APPRAISED
DEJECTEDLY	BELLIGERENTLY	INDIGNATION	ASHAMEDLY	SUBSIDED
MONOTONOUS	RELUCTANTLY	GESTURED	MEAGER	IMPRESSIVELY

Of Mice and Men Vocabulary

PANTOMIME	DEROGATORY	DISARMING	SUBDUED	COMPLACENTLY
PROFOUND	PERSUASIVE	CONSOLED	QUIVERING	MOROSELY
APPREHENSIVE	SNIVELED	FREE SPACE	CONTEMPLATED	CONTORTED
MOLLIFIED	CONTEMPTUOUSLY	ENTRANCED	ANGUISHED	IMPRESSIVELY
MEAGER	GESTURED	RELUCTANTLY	MONOTONOUS	SUBSIDED

Of Mice and Men Vocabulary

MIMICKING	PRECEDE	APPRAISED	COMPLACENTLY	CONSOLED
ASHAMEDLY	RELUCTANTLY	IMPRESSIVELY	DEROGATORY	WRITHED
PLAINTIVELY	SUBSIDED	FREE SPACE	ENTRANCED	SULLENNESS
GESTURED	INDIGNATION	SNIVELED	SULKILY	REPREHENSIBLE
RETORTED	DISARMING	DEJECTEDLY	BEWILDERED	CONTEMPLATED

Of Mice and Men Vocabulary

PANTOMIME	PERSUASIVE	CONCEALING	SUBDUED	MEAGER
QUIVERING	MAULED	MONOTONOUS	CONTORTED	BEMUSED
SKEPTICALLY	CONTEMPTUOUSLY	FREE SPACE	MOLLIFIED	OMINOUSLY
PROFOUND	CONFIDED	BELLIGERENTLY	MOROSELY	CONTEMPLATED
BEWILDERED	DEJECTEDLY	DISARMING	RETORTED	REPREHENSIBLE

Of Mice and Men Vocabulary

BEMUSED	MAULED	RETORTED	APPRAISED	SUBSIDED
SULLENNESS	ANGUISHED	BELLIGERENTLY	QUIVERING	APPREHENSIVE
SUBDUED	CONFIDED	FREE SPACE	DEROGATORY	CONTEMPTUOUSLY
SULKILY	MOROSELY	SKEPTICALLY	PRECEDE	CONCEALING
GESTURED	CONTEMPLATED	MEAGER	DEJECTEDLY	REPREHENSIBLE

Of Mice and Men Vocabulary

ENTRANCED	PROFOUND	INDIGNATION	MONOTONOUS	MOLLIFIED
IMPRESSIVELY	PLAINTIVELY	PANTOMIME	COMPLACENTLY	CONTORTED
BEWILDERED	SNIVELED	FREE SPACE	MIMICKING	OMINOUSLY
DISARMING	PERSUASIVE	RELUCTANTLY	ASHAMEDLY	REPREHENSIBLE
DEJECTEDLY	MEAGER	CONTEMPLATED	GESTURED	CONCEALING

Of Mice and Men Vocabulary

DEJECTEDLY	PLAINTIVELY	MONOTONOUS	IMPRESSIVELY	REPREHENSIBLE
CONSOLED	SULLENNESS	BELLIGERENTLY	ENTRANCED	RETORTED
SUBDUED	QUIVERING	FREE SPACE	SNIVELED	CONTORTED
SUBSIDED	GESTURED	APPREHENSIVE	MEAGER	MOLLIFIED
CONTEMPTUOUSLY	MOROSELY	PROFOUND	PRECEDE	PERSUASIVE

Of Mice and Men Vocabulary

BEMUSED	CONTEMPLATED	CONCEALING	MAULED	OMINOUSLY
SKEPTICALLY	BEWILDERED	INDIGNATION	COMPLACENTLY	ASHAMEDLY
RELUCTANTLY	DISARMING	FREE SPACE	DEROGATORY	MIMICKING
APPRAISED	SULKILY	ANGUISHED	CONFIDED	PERSUASIVE
PRECEDE	PROFOUND	MOROSELY	CONTEMPTUOUSLY	MOLLIFIED

Of Mice and Men Vocabulary

DISARMING	ANGUISHED	QUIVERING	CONTEMPLATED	BELLIGERENTLY
APPREHENSIVE	PLAINTIVELY	CONTEMPTUOUSLY	DEJECTEDLY	BEMUSED
BEWILDERED	CONSOLED	FREE SPACE	OMINOUSLY	MAULED
RELUCTANTLY	SUBDUED	PERSUASIVE	WRITHED	SULLENNESS
SNIVELED	SULKILY	ASHAMEDLY	GESTURED	CONTORTED

Of Mice and Men Vocabulary

APPRAISED	REPREHENSIBLE	MIMICKING	SKEPTICALLY	IMPRESSIVELY
SUBSIDED	PANTOMIME	COMPLACENTLY	RETORTED	CONCEALING
INDIGNATION	ENTRANCED	FREE SPACE	PRECEDE	MONOTONOUS
PROFOUND	MOLLIFIED	CONFIDED	MOROSELY	CONTORTED
GESTURED	ASHAMEDLY	SULKILY	SNIVELED	SULLENNESS

Of Mice and Men Vocabulary

SKEPTICALLY	INDIGNATION	MIMICKING	DEROGATORY	APPRAISED
BELLIGERENTLY	CONCEALING	SUBSIDED	IMPRESSIVELY	SULKILY
REPREHENSIBLE	ANGUISHED	FREE SPACE	MOLLIFIED	DEJECTEDLY
WRITHED	PLAINTIVELY	PRECEDE	BEWILDERED	BEMUSED
CONTEMPTUOUSLY	CONSOLED	CONTEMPLATED	MAULED	CONTORTED

Of Mice and Men Vocabulary

MONOTONOUS	ENTRANCED	SUBDUED	GESTURED	COMPLACENTLY
OMINOUSLY	MOROSELY	QUIVERING	MEAGER	DISARMING
SNIVELED	RETORTED	FREE SPACE	APPREHENSIVE	PERSUASIVE
SULLENNESS	RELUCTANTLY	PANTOMIME	PROFOUND	CONTORTED
MAULED	CONTEMPLATED	CONSOLED	CONTEMPTUOUSLY	BEMUSED

Of Mice and Men Vocabulary

SULKILY	SUBSIDED	PROFOUND	MAULED	MOLLIFIED
ASHAMEDLY	PERSUASIVE	SKEPTICALLY	OMINOUSLY	RELUCTANTLY
MEAGER	DISARMING	FREE SPACE	CONCEALING	ANGUISHED
BELLIGERENTLY	DEROGATORY	CONTORTED	REPREHENSIBLE	BEWILDERED
BEMUSED	CONTEMPTUOUSLY	SNIVELED	APPREHENSIVE	ENTRANCED

Of Mice and Men Vocabulary

APPRAISED	SULLENNESS	INDIGNATION	COMPLACENTLY	MIMICKING
MOROSELY	CONSOLED	PANTOMIME	PRECEDE	GESTURED
WRITHED	MONOTONOUS	FREE SPACE	PLAINTIVELY	SUBDUED
CONTEMPLATED	DEJECTEDLY	QUIVERING	IMPRESSIVELY	ENTRANCED
APPREHENSIVE	SNIVELED	CONTEMPTUOUSLY	BEMUSED	BEWILDERED

Of Mice and Men Vocabulary

SNIVELED	CONCEALING	DISARMING	BELLIGERENTLY	DEROGATORY
QUIVERING	BEMUSED	APPRAISED	IMPRESSIVELY	GESTURED
SULLENNESS	SUBSIDED	FREE SPACE	ENTRANCED	REPREHENSIBLE
RELUCTANTLY	CONTEMPLATED	CONSOLED	SKEPTICALLY	COMPLACENTLY
MOROSELY	SULKILY	OMINOUSLY	RETORTED	ASHAMEDLY

Of Mice and Men Vocabulary

DEJECTEDLY	ANGUISHED	CONTEMPTUOUSLY	PRECEDE	MIMICKING
CONTORTED	BEWILDERED	PROFOUND	MOLLIFIED	MEAGER
PLAINTIVELY	CONFIDED	FREE SPACE	MONOTONOUS	APPREHENSIVE
SUBDUED	PERSUASIVE	MAULED	INDIGNATION	ASHAMEDLY
RETORTED	OMINOUSLY	SULKILY	MOROSELY	COMPLACENTLY

Of Mice and Men Vocabulary

ASHAMEDLY	PRECEDE	RETORTED	CONFIDED	ENTRANCED
INDIGNATION	MONOTONOUS	PROFOUND	SNIVELED	SUBDUED
MAULED	MEAGER	FREE SPACE	PLAINTIVELY	WRITHED
REPREHENSIBLE	OMINOUSLY	RELUCTANTLY	BEWILDERED	ANGUISHED
COMPLACENTLY	IMPRESSIVELY	SUBSIDED	SULKILY	DEJECTEDLY

Of Mice and Men Vocabulary

MOLLIFIED	APPREHENSIVE	BEMUSED	PANTOMIME	APPRAISED
CONCEALING	MIMICKING	CONTORTED	MOROSELY	CONTEMPTUOUSLY
GESTURED	CONSOLED	FREE SPACE	DISARMING	PERSUASIVE
SULLENNESS	SKEPTICALLY	QUIVERING	BELLIGERENTLY	DEJECTEDLY
SULKILY	SUBSIDED	IMPRESSIVELY	COMPLACENTLY	ANGUISHED

Of Mice and Men Vocabulary

ANGUISHED	CONTEMPLATED	MAULED	DEROGATORY	BEWILDERED
CONFIDED	CONSOLED	SULLENNESS	APPREHENSIVE	MOROSELY
QUIVERING	DEJECTEDLY	FREE SPACE	WRITHED	PLAINTIVELY
INDIGNATION	REPREHENSIBLE	DISARMING	SUBSIDED	GESTURED
RETORTED	CONTORTED	IMPRESSIVELY	PRECEDE	APPRAISED

Of Mice and Men Vocabulary

PERSUASIVE	PROFOUND	OMINOUSLY	ENTRANCED	MONOTONOUS
CONTEMPTUOUSLY	RELUCTANTLY	ASHAMEDLY	PANTOMIME	BEMUSED
SNIVELED	MOLLIFIED	FREE SPACE	SKEPTICALLY	BELLIGERENTLY
COMPLACENTLY	MEAGER	SUBDUED	CONCEALING	APPRAISED
PRECEDE	IMPRESSIVELY	CONTORTED	RETORTED	GESTURED

Of Mice and Men Vocabulary

MEAGER	MONOTONOUS	DEJECTEDLY	ASHAMEDLY	BEWILDERED
BELLIGERENTLY	SUBDUED	CONTEMPLATED	CONTEMPTUOUSLY	WRITHED
SULLENNESS	PANTOMIME	FREE SPACE	RETORTED	IMPRESSIVELY
QUIVERING	ANGUISHED	SNIVELED	CONTORTED	CONFIDED
GESTURED	CONSOLED	MAULED	CONCEALING	APPRAISED

Of Mice and Men Vocabulary

ENTRANCED	MIMICKING	APPREHENSIVE	REPREHENSIBLE	DISARMING
BEMUSED	MOLLIFIED	SULKILY	PRECEDE	SKEPTICALLY
RELUCTANTLY	PERSUASIVE	FREE SPACE	INDIGNATION	PLAINTIVELY
SUBSIDED	OMINOUSLY	DEROGATORY	MOROSELY	APPRAISED
CONCEALING	MAULED	CONSOLED	GESTURED	CONFIDED

Of Mice and Men Vocabulary

SUBSIDED	PROFOUND	SUBDUED	DEJECTEDLY	COMPLACENTLY
SULKILY	ENTRANCED	BEWILDERED	BELLIGERENTLY	PANTOMIME
ANGUISHED	PLAINTIVELY	FREE SPACE	DEROGATORY	MOROSELY
MOLLIFIED	APPRAISED	CONTORTED	SKEPTICALLY	CONCEALING
QUIVERING	REPREHENSIBLE	MAULED	GESTURED	MONOTONOUS

Of Mice and Men Vocabulary

MEAGER	PRECEDE	DISARMING	IMPRESSIVELY	RETORTED
INDIGNATION	CONTEMPTUOUSLY	MIMICKING	CONSOLED	BEMUSED
SULLENNESS	RELUCTANTLY	FREE SPACE	CONFIDED	SNIVELED
CONTEMPLATED	WRITHED	PERSUASIVE	ASHAMEDLY	MONOTONOUS
GESTURED	MAULED	REPREHENSIBLE	QUIVERING	CONCEALING

www.ingramcontent.com/pod-product-compliance
Lightning Source LLC
Chambersburg PA
CBHW081457070526
44586CB00019B/2393